Santiago Calatrava

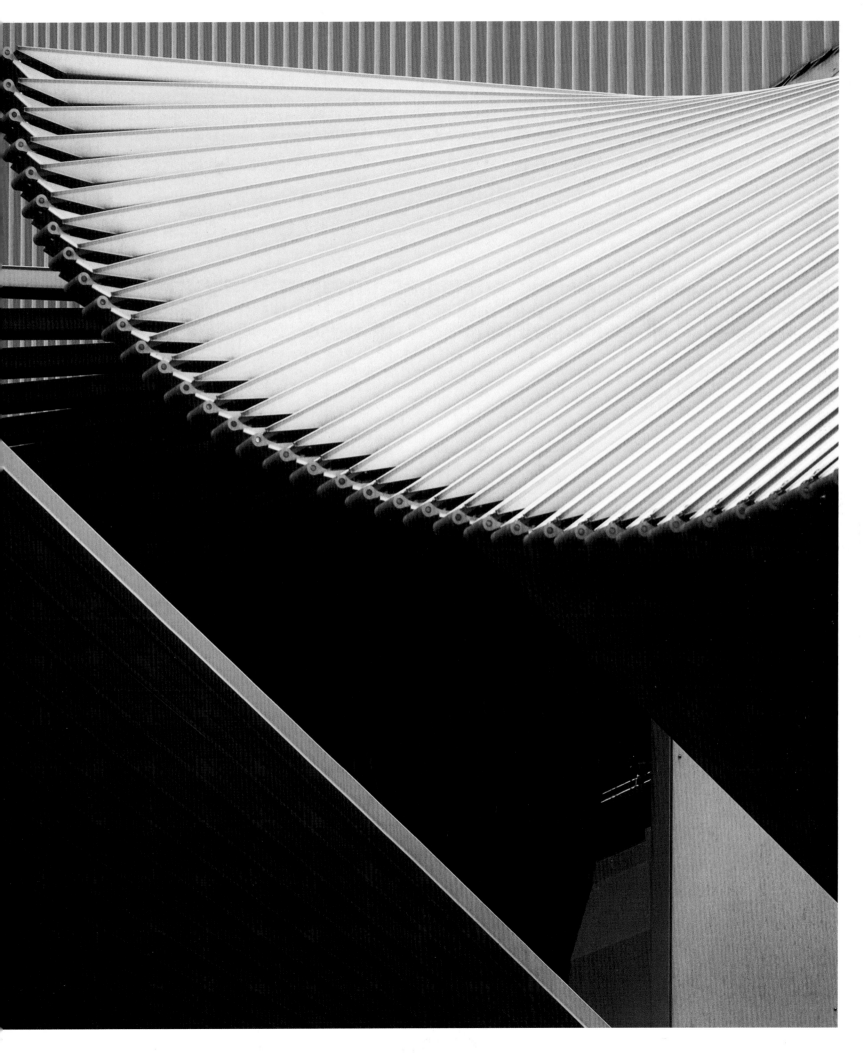

Alexander Tzonis

Santiago Calatrava | The Complete Works

First published in the United States of America by
Rizzoli International Publications, Inc.
300 Park Avenue South
New York, NY 10010
www.rizzoliusa.com

2004 2005 2006 2007 / 10 9 8 7 6 5 4 3 2 1

ISBN: 0-8478-2641-4
Library of Congress Control Number: 2004094978

Research Assistant: Rebeca Caso Donadei
Design by Binocular, New York
Printed in Italy

Jacket front: Milwaukee Art Museum, Milwaukee,
Wisconsin; jacket back: Pont d'Orléans, Orléans,
France; page 2: Ernsting Warehouse, Coesfeld-Lette,
Germany; page 4: Alamillo Bridge, Seville, Spain; page
6: Lyons Airport Station, Satolas (Lyons), France; page
8: Volantin Footbridge, Bilbao, Spain; page 10: Tenerife
Concert Hall, Tenerife, Canary Islands, Spain; page 12:
City of Arts and Sciences Planetarium, Valencia, Spain;
page 14: Oriente Station, Lisbon, Portugal; page 16:
Milwaukee Art Museum, Milwaukee, Wisconsin; page
18: Pont d'Orléans, Orléans, France; page 20: Tenerife
Concert Hall, Tenerife, Canary Islands, Spain

Contents

27   Acknowledgments

31   Prologue: The Persistence of Flying

39   Chapter 1 | Constructing Foundations, Unfolding Horizons

61   Chapter 2 | Pregnant Moments, Nascent Structures

113   Chapter 3 | Metamorphoses and Heuristic Dreams

141   Chapter 4 | Morphogenetic Movements

251   Chapter 5 | Spinozian Sculptures

283   Chapter 6 | Landmarking

357   Chapter 7 | Forms of the Body and the Spirit

373   Epilogue: White Time

393   Notes

397   Bibliography

400   Biography

409   Catalogue Raisonné

432   Photography Credits

Featured Project List

64 Roof for the IBA Squash Hall
Berlin, Germany
1979

66 Ernsting Warehouse
Coesfeld-Lette, Germany
1983–85

72 Stadelhofen Railway Station
Zurich, Switzerland
1983–90

86 Wohlen High School
Wohlen, Switzerland
1983–88

94 Lucerne Station Hall
Lucerne, Switzerland
1983–89

98 Bärenmatte Community Center
Suhr, Switzerland
1984–88

102 Caballeros Footbridge
Lerida, Spain
1985

104 Bach de Roda Bridge
Barcelona, Spain
1985–87

110 Tabourettli Theater
Basel, Switzerland
1986–87

142 BCE Place
Toronto, Canada
1987–92

146 Alamillo Bridge
Seville, Spain
1987–92

150 Lusitania Bridge
Mérida, Spain
1988–91

156 Collserola Telecommunications Tower
Barcelona, Spain
1988

158 Montjuic Telecommunications Tower
Barcelona, Spain
1989–92

162 Bauschänzli Restaurant
Zurich, Switzerland
1988

164 Emergency Services Center
St. Gallen, Switzerland
1988–98

164 Pfalzkeller Gallery
St. Gallen, Switzerland
1988–98

170 Zurich University Law Faculty
Zurich, Switzerland
1989–2004

172   CH-91 Pavilion
Lucerne, Switzerland
1989

174   Lyons Airport Station
Satolas (Lyons), France
1989–94

184   Puerto Bridge
Ondarroa, Spain
1989–91

188   La Devesa Footbridge
Ripoll, Spain
1989–91

192   Volantin Footbridge
Bilbao, Spain
1990–97

196   Sondica Airport
Bilbao, Spain
1990–2000

202   Tenerife Concert Hall
Tenerife, Canary Islands, Spain
1991–2003

210   Kuwait Pavilion
Seville, Spain
1991–92

216   City of Arts and Sciences
Valencia, Spain
1991–96

226   Alameda Bridge and Underground Station
Valencia, Spain
1991–95

230   Cathedral of St. John the Divine
New York City
1991

234   Spandau Station
Berlin, Germany
1991

236   Jahn Olympic Sports Complex
Berlin, Germany
1991

238   Reichstag
Berlin, Germany
1992

240   Alcoy Community Hall
Alcoy, Spain
1992–95

246   Trinity Footbridge
Salford, England
1993–95

248   Sondica Airport Control Tower
Bilbao, Spain
1993–96

270   Swissbau Pavilion
Basel, Switzerland
1988

272   *Shadow Machine*, *Wave*, and *Weed*
New York City and Venice, Italy
1992–93

284   Oriente Station
Lisbon, Portugal
1993–98

290   Milwaukee Art Museum
Milwaukee, Wisconsin
1994–2001

304   Manrique Footbridge
Murcia, Spain
1994–99

304   Embankment Renaissance Footbridge
Bedford, England
1995

304   Quarto Ponte sul Canal Grande
Venice, Italy
1996–

308   Church of the Year 2000
Rome, Italy
1996

310   Valencia Opera House
Valencia, Spain
1996–2004

316   Pont d'Orléans
Orléans, France
1996–2000

320   Pont des Guillemins
Liège, Belgium
1998–2000

322   La Rioja Bodegas Ysios Winery
La Guardia, Spain
1998–2001

328   Puente de la Mujer
Buenos Aires, Argentina
1998–2001

332   Turning Torso Apartment Tower
Malmö, Sweden
1999–2005

334   Christ the Light Cathedral
Oakland, California
2000

336   Master Plan for the 2004 Olympic and
Paralympic Games
Athens, Greece
2001–4

346   Expansion Plan for the
Museo dell'Opera del Duomo
Florence, Italy
2002–

348   Light Rail Train Bridge
Jerusalem, Israel
2002–

374   80 South Street Tower
New York City
2000–

379   World Trade Center Transportation Hub
New York City
2003–

Acknowledgments

I wish to acknowledge my debt to people with whom I worked in the past on the architecture of Santiago Calatrava: Anthony Tischauser, Rifca Hashimshony, Micha Levin, and especially Liane Lefaivre.

Santiago and Tina Calatrava were most generous in offering their collaboration. I am thankful for their care and inspiration. Special thanks also to the staff of Santiago Calatrava, S.A., and to Kim Marangoni and Christof Mühle-mann. This book benefited from discussions with Robert Berwick, Ovadia Salama, Dimitri Balamotis, Uri Shetrit, and Karen Bloch.

I owe many thanks to Ron Broadhurst, my editor at Rizzoli, and to David Morton and Charles Miers for their effective support. Special thanks to all members of the Design Knowledge Systems Research Center of TUD, Jan Willem Ter Steege, Asaf Friedman, my secretary Janneke Arkesteijn, and in particular to Rebeca Caso Donadei, research assistant for the book.

Throughout the years and during the writing of this book, Professor F.H. Schroeder's friend-ship was a great encouragement; this book is dedicated to him.

Santiago Calatrava

Prologue | The Persistence of Flying

On Thursday, January 22, 2004, the design for the World Trade Center Transportation Hub of the Port Authority of New York and New Jersey, or PATH terminal, was released by the Downtown Design Partnership in association with Santiago Calatrava, in essence the "author" of the design. The public unveiling of the project, which was estimated to cost approximately $2 billion, took place in the Winter Garden of the World Financial Center at Battery Park City. It was the first of a series of projects marking the renaissance of Ground Zero, as the site of the terrible ruins of September 11, 2001, came to be known. Calatrava's scheme was received with universal acclaim. Loud applause, a literal ovation, was the audience's response to Calatrava's presentation. An equally enthusiastic reaction was registered by New York Governor George Pataki and the officials of the Port Authority of New York and New Jersey, the builders of the terminal. And, according to the New York Times, the chairman of the city's Landmarks Preservation Commission, Robert B. Tierney, proposed on the spot to "preemptively landmark" the structure.[1] Similar was the response of the relatives and friends of the victims of September 11, the comments of fellow architects, including Daniel Libeskind (the chief planner of the site), and the writers who covered the public presentation.

It was a rare day of excitement and unity for the people of New York, introducing a sense of optimism to the traumatized city and offering a palliative to the mood of dispute, doubt, and gloom. The pristine model of the project itself radiated a rare aura of technical perfection, aesthetic rightness, and epic public monumentality. But it also appeared strange, uncommon, and enigmatic. To explain his idea of the station, Calatrava addressed issues ranging from engineering to the the meaning of public works for the hardworking population of the city, as well as the city's almost forgotten qualities of Mediterranean light and its long tradition of masterpieces of public architecture such as the old Pennsylvania Station and Grand Central Terminal. Then, in front of the transfixed audience, Calatrava opened his drawing kit and quickly sketched the outline of the new terminal, looking something like an underground cathedral, and over it a giant bird, oversize like a Claes Oldenburg object in the midst of a dense public space, a bird let free by a child, opening its wings to fly into the air.

Axonometric drawings
of a folding structure

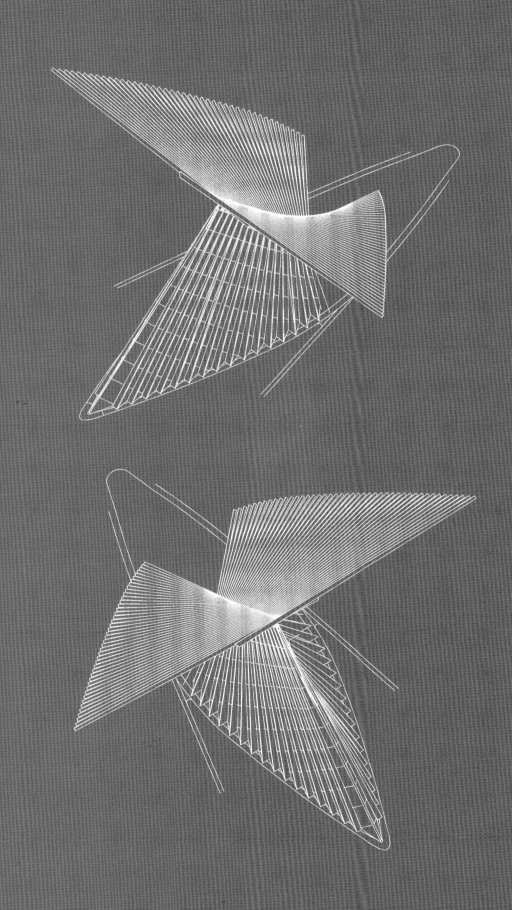

It was an act of masterful public drama that the politicians were quick to grasp and together with the audience to join in. It was not the first time that Calatrava performed in this manner, but in the context of the time and place it was most felicitous. New Yorkers have a long tradition of public drama. However, not far from the ruins of Ground Zero, where the ceremony was taking place, this display of knowledge, creativity, and will was, as in an ancient drama, genuinely cathartic.

Without doubt, Calatrava's success in New York was the result of being the right person in the right place at the right time. However, beyond lucky coincidences, Calatrava's success was the result of the special qualities that his design demonstrated. The project worked on many levels simultaneously: it was a public place, an urban monument, a metropolitan megamachine, and a work of art. The importance of this synthesis was something that even a layman could understand, a quality that is as desirable as it is rare.

Indeed, there are very few designers who can be called universal in our time, an era dominated by division and specialization, turning fragments of knowledge and culture into idols. Santiago Calatrava is one of these. In a unique manner, he has resisted insular divisions without becoming an amateur. He has defied specialization while deepening his understanding of specific problems. His design quest cuts across intellectual and institutional boundaries erected between science, technology, and art, his artifacts overcome the chasm separating knowing, doing, and inquiring.

A typical Calatrava structure is an intelligent technological solution, an elegant answer to a given functional problem. Functional optimality, however, is not the single objective of his structures. Beyond (but *not* against) optimal technology, the structures explain and instruct. Yet they are not just didactic demonstrations. Behind their materials and shapes is a deeper cognitive, poetic, and moral significance. They comment, confront, and awake consciousness through enigma, paradox, even humor. They turn the technological answers into new questions. They invite us to move on, recalling Galileo's famous utterance before the dogmatists of his own day: "*Eppur' si muove* (And yet it does move)."

As a maker of structures, Calatrava is preoccupied with making things stand. We do not expect a good structure to change shape, break loose, crack, rupture, snap, come apart, overturn, or, least of all, collapse. The very idea of a structure is felt to be synonymous with

World Trade Center
Transportation Hub,
New York, ground-level
plan of proposal

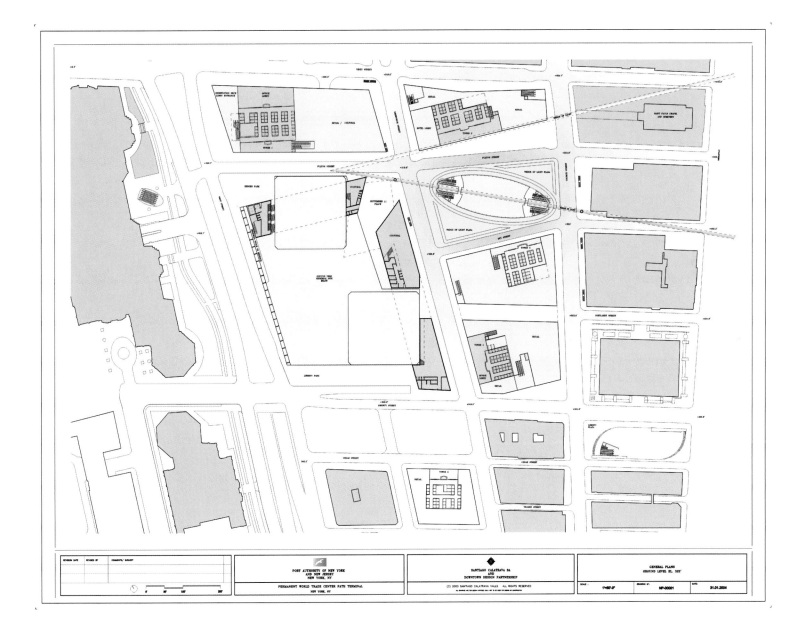

permanence, solidity, and the rigid organization of elements. Intuitively, movement is the last thing one tends to associate with built structures. Yet, looking at Calatrava's structures, their acrobatic gestures, their dancerlike, falling/flying postures, it appears that the structures incorporate movement and that Calatrava, technologically or figuratively, literally or metaphorically, explicitly or implicitly, tries to negate stasis rather than preserve it.

What transpired on January 22, 2004, during the unveiling of the scheme for the World Trade Center Transportation Hub was an effort to give back movement to structures, or, to paraphrase French philosopher Henri Bergson, to awake the chrysalis at the heart of his structures and restore their mobility, their élan vital, to identify their "reality in [their] mobility . . . in which novelty is constantly springing forth and evolution is creative."[2] It is this commitment to life that made

the greatest impression on the audience present for the ceremony on January 22, and on the wider audience who viewed coverage of the event the following day.

World Trade Center
Transportation Hub,
New York, computer
rendering

Chapter 1 | Constructing Foundations, Unfolding Horizons

Santiago Calatrava was born in Benimamet, a small village near Valencia, Spain, on July 28, 1951. He received his basic education in Valencia, a once thriving royal city. Founded by the Greeks, it was occupied by Romans, Arabs, Moors, and Goths, and in the thirteenth century hosted a large and vibrant Jewish population. Despite its royal past, Valencia played an important role in numerous republican uprisings during the nineteenth and twentieth centuries. It was here that the last remnants of the Republican Party found refuge and ultimately surrendered, after the fall of Catalonia to the Franco army in 1939. By then Valencia had declined into a regional, agrarian center, but its rich past was preserved in its architectural monuments, particularly in the fifteenth-century Lonja de la Seda, the hall of the bourse, at the Plaza del Mercado. Of the buildings in the historical center of the city, it was the Lonja with its elegant tall columns resembling a forest of palm trees that most impressed young Santiago when he was taken for a walk there by his father. Later, in an interview with Liane Lefaivre, he recalled the effect Lonja had on his work as a model par excellence of "anti-gravitational space."[1]

Calatrava's serious involvement with design began early, when he was enrolled at the age of eight in the Valencia School of Arts and Crafts to learn drawing and painting. When he was thirteen, his mother, eager to broaden his horizons, arranged for him to travel as an exchange student to Paris ostensibly to learn French but also to experience the great works of art. Four years later she sent him to Zurich, this time to learn German. Santiago returned to Paris after finishing high school in June 1968 with the intention to study at the École des Beaux-Arts, only to find himself in the midst of the famous student revolt that had shut all universities. As Lawrence Stone, chairman of the history department of Princeton University, wrote, the students disrupted university functions to redefine its identity from a conformist institution to one whose function would be "for the subversion of the society."[2] In reality what the students meant by "subversion" mainly had cultural implications. As Steven Spender observed in his *Year of the Young Rebels* (1968), the students had risen against "the rule of things" and, to quote the famous article published at that time by *Le Monde*, "Imagination Is Revolution," had come to regard "every view which is not strange as false."

Determined not to waste any time, Calatrava returned to Valencia to enter the School of Arts and Crafts. However, the defiant "creative" spirit of May 1968 forever marked his development. But his particular spirit of revolt had to do less with Allen Ginsberg and more with the regeneration of the original avant-garde of Matisse,

Picasso, and Buñuel. Santiago continued to study at the School of Arts and Crafts only for the rest of the academic year. By then it was clear in his mind that it was architecture he wanted to study. In a laconic, frank application statement addressed to the Escuela Técnica Superior de Arquitectura de Valencia he wrote:

The reasons why I want to study architecture are the following:

I am interested in drawing.

I always felt excitement for artistic matters.

I think I have capabilities for the study and development of this profession.

I have high hopes for this career and I expect that with my work and resilience I will surmount the weaknesses in education and abilities that I have now.

I also think that it is here that I will benefit society the most for I am sure that I will be able to practice this career with enthusiasm and love.

Apart from giving emphasis to "work" and "artistic matters" rather than talent, the document is interesting because it considers drawing to be an essential part of architecture while it remains silent about technical aspects. Calatrava entered the school of architecture bringing with him not only the basic skills of drawing, but also the experience of a special "five points" exercise, which is thought to have been invented by Goya. The student is given five points and is asked to inscribe within them a human figure. The fascinating aspect of this exercise is that it trains the student to conceive the arrangement of the position of figure within given constraints, the "five points." For Calatrava the exercise became a mechanism to stimulate the invention of original forms. But it also turned into a paradigm for grasping the problem routinely faced by engineers: to lay out a structure within specific spatial constraints.

Calatrava enrolled in the Escuela Técnica Superior de Arquitectura de Valencia in fall 1969, ironically just in time for the impact of the Parisian revolt to be felt in Valencia. Although not so fierce as in Paris, the effect of May 1968 in Valencia was strong enough to disrupt the regular program of education of the school of architecture. As in other parts of Europe and the United States at that time, several students began to propose "alternative" types of education. On one hand the situation was very frustrating for Calatrava, thirsty as he was to be instructed in the discipline of architecture. On the other, he was very much in agreement that to be drilled in the dogma of mainstream design practice was useless, if not destructive. The prospect of self-education fit his self-propelled temperament as it had for Le Corbusier, the great rebel of the old avant-garde, who was to a great extent an autodidact. Calatrava eagerly developed with other students a course of

The "five points" exercise from young Calatrava's sketchbooks

study involving visiting and documenting Iberian vernacular structures as opposed to official or mainstream architecture. For Spanish students and young architects involvement with this non-monumental architecture was itself an act of defiance. For Calatrava contact with the freshness, directness, and functionality of these works only reinforced the belief he was already forming in his mind, that serious education implied self-imposed discipline and self-defined goals rather than passive acceptance of received information. Following this direction he included in his schedule a visit to Le Corbusier's Chapel of Notre Dame du Haut at Ronchamp, France. Ronchamp was commissioned the year Calatrava was born and today it is universally acclaimed as a modern classic. Yet major critics at the time of its construction called its forms a "puzzle" or a "scandal." For Calatrava, however, it was simply an amazing configuration of uncanny shapes. He had a similar reac-

tion to the propellerlike, spiral external staircase of Le Corbusier's Unité d'habitation, Marseilles, France, which he saw in a small book on Le Corbusier's work. He immediately became obsessed with the secret of their creation and he energetically tried to capture their form, which for him meant representing it. In many respects this impulse is reminiscent of Le Corbusier's remarks in *New World of Space* (1948) regarding his sketching and photographing buildings during his own educational travels in the Balkans and Mediterranean, where he describes drawing as "observing, discovering . . . inventing, and creating."[3]

How could one represent the complex, seemingly indescribable, formless Ronchamp and the equally indescribable forms of Spanish folk architecture? Freehand sketching did not seem sufficient to grasp their underlying spatial construction. Here science stepped in to rescue the perplexed Calatrava, specifically the science

of descriptive geometry. Working from an academic text, Calatrava tried to teach himself the basics of descriptive geometry while drawing geometrically constructed perspectives of the two buildings. Certainly descriptive geometry could not reveal the "secret" of the spatial arrangement of Ronchamp, but the experience of trying to represent through rational descriptive geometry the explosive world of the building gave Calatrava a taste of the power of analytical tools and confidence in their potential. To advance his knowledge of such tools, a few years later, in 1974, having graduated as an architect and having taken a postgraduate course in urbanism, Calatrava left Valencia for Zurich. There he enrolled as a student in the department of civil engineering at the Swiss Federal Institute of Technology (ETH).

After his graduation in 1979, Calatrava immediately started working as an assistant at

This page: Calatrava's sketch of Notre Dame du Haut, Ronchamp, by Le Corbusier. Opposite: Milwaukee Art Museum, a moving structure

the Institute for Building Statics and Construction and Aerodynamics and Lightweight Construction while at the same time beginning work on his doctoral thesis, *On the Foldability of Space Frames*.

Looking at the voluminous mathematical symbols and elaborate abstract physical models included in the dissertation, completed in 1981 when Calatrava was still under thirty, one may wonder why a person with such creative capabilities in designing with the same ease buildings, bridges, furniture, and sculpture, imposed on himself the burden of such rigorous intellectual labor. Why did he devote such a decisive period of his life making calculations and mechanical contraptions? Was he uncertain about the power of his imagination and delaying his commitment to design?

The question however makes sense only if one adheres to the popular "romantic" view that considers creative design to be an uncanny miracle defying any explication, ignoring the cognitive mechanisms of the creative process. According to this view *analytical* research is of no use to ingenious designers who need only inspiration and for whom, as the etymology of the word *inspire* suggests, conceiving schemes is like breathing. In other words the creative shaping of unknown forms is effortless, spontaneous, and without any preparation: new schemes emerge in the brain like lightning, a view that appears to be confirmed when one witnesses Calatrava designing in public as he did at the presentation of his proposal for the World Trade Center Transportation Hub.

From the cognitive point of view, however, Calatrava was constructing with his dissertation a solid foundation to sustain and enhance the generation of his future design schemes. The dissertation explains, in part, the ease and freedom with which he would produce novel artifacts in the years to come. It also sheds light on how analysis plays a major role in creative design.

As the title of the dissertation, *On the Foldability of Space Frames*, suggests, the question Calatrava set up to answer through this investigation was how one can design complex structures, more specifically frame structures, that could move and thereby be transformed, that is, change from one shape into another without changing the way the pieces were joined together. In the back of his mind was still the question of how to represent complex surfaces using structures that move. The two questions seem independent of one another, but their interrelationship was understood by Calatrava from the beginning.

The goal of the dissertation, the study of frame structures that could move, implied the study of the constraints that permit these frames to open, stretch flat, form an umbrella-like dome, collapse, and close to shrink into a compact rod. This was a problem unfamiliar to most architects, who were traditionally preoccupied with stable and immobile structures; structures that move, despite the obvious functionality they offer, did not attract their attention. It was only during the 1960s that moving structures had begun to play a significant role in the design of roofs, as, for example, in the case of the Civic Auditorium in Pittsburgh, Pennsylvania, built in 1961 with a retractable roof designed by James A. Mitchell and Dahlen K. Ritchey. During the same period members of the British group Archigram took a more visionary approach inspired by R. Buckminster Fuller's pre–World War II work, though Fuller did not pursue the problem systematically. Archigram was also motivated by designs for large-scale machines with folding parts, such as cranes, excavation shovels, and other construction equipment, and their ideas were primarily visionary and not intended for practical application. Within the academic framework in the United States, William Zuk at the University of Virginia carried out design exercises that focused on folding structures, as did Roger H. Clark at North Carolina State University. But their efforts were fragmentary and did not lead to a coherent body of knowledge.

Another important precedent for Calatrava's research was the work carried out by the American space program, whose engineers had been designing equipment since the 1960s for space missions with the goal of extended periods of interplanetary travel. These missions required vehicles with a variety of instruments: solar energy collectors, reflectors for communication antennas, sensors, radio-frequency lenses, meteorite shields, and telescopes. The conditions under which such space instruments had to operate were completely new, and therefore a wholly original set of design requirements had to be met. Like a sail, each instrument required a large surface area that could be packed tightly into a compact volume and unpacked again when it was needed. In other words these instruments had to be collapsible into a compressed package for transportation to space and also reliably deployable onto a spread-out plane for operation in orbit. Also during the 1960s, the Astro Research Corporation conducted studies to design a simple, large orbiting radio telescope structure. The scheme was broken down into bracing elements, joints, a deploying motor, and a column that could be folded into a canister. More studies followed, and by 1975 the National Aeronautics and Space Administration (NASA) had developed a more complex scheme for a foldable and sequentially deployable structure intended to support a surface for energy

Overleaf: Foldable frame structure illustrations from Calatrava's dissertation, *On the Foldability of Space Frames*

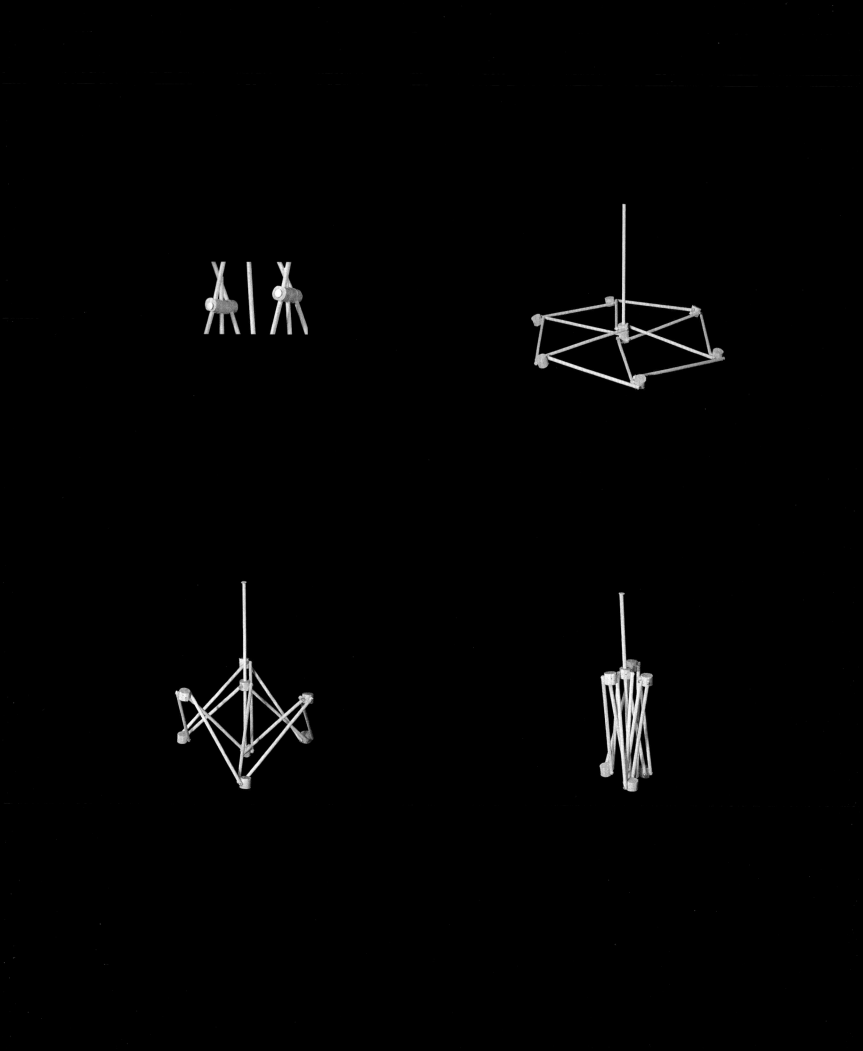

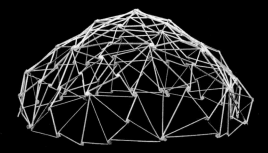

collectors. It was made out of a rigid, sectioned, hinged rim structure braced with spokes joined to a shared hub. The device could be transformed from a linear shape into a three-dimensional stellate form, or into a two-dimensional regular polygon. The multisided rim could be opened to the extent that the "rim-couples" fanned out radially from the axis of the central hub. The device also included torques at the hinges, which either controlled spokes or synchronized motors. These projects, largely unknown among building engineers, were important cutting-edge precedents with which Calatrava quickly became familiar.

Like the folding structures of NASA, Calatrava's folding structures for buildings had the same criteria for success: their efficiency depended on their compactness, their open surface being as wide as possible, and their folded volume as small as possible. Their effectiveness rested on the coordination of the sweep angle of their rods in movement, which in turn depended on articulating joints so that they could move without obstructing each other. The problem was first geometrical (representing the transformation of the shape of the structure from a folded to an open one or vice versa), then mechanical (making the parts of a structure move from one position to another), and, finally, static (ensuring the stability of the structure).

Contrary to the moving roofs and machine parts mentioned above as well as NASA's research to design specific artifacts and customized solutions for single problems, Calatrava's ambition was to develop a body of knowledge that could solve the problem generically, to develop, if not a real theory, at least a general approach that could grasp the many facets of folding structures. This interest in developing a design tool to enhance the conception of many schemes for a wide range of products to come was the point of generation for his dissertation.[4]

This page: Suspended pool, an early project at the ETH Zurich. Opposite: Pool suspended by cables

Given the novelty of the subject, Calatrava decided to define his thesis as a multidisciplinary research project, so that his evaluation committee included a general supervisor, Herbert E. Kramel (also an architect) and experts from several faculties, such as Robert Kaeser (aircraft statics) and Hans Brauchli (mathematics). Brauchli was in fact already involved with similar mathematical problems. To develop this system Calatrava recruited a branch of mathematics known as the theory of transformations, which deals with a class of geometrical constructions applied in the design of a family of mechanical devices called linkages. Following this paradigm, foldable frame structures were represented as sets of bars connected by joints with properties of stability and foldability. The first step was to break down the problem into modeling the geometrical transformation of three-dimensional frames and articulating the mechanical connectors in the joints required for this sequential

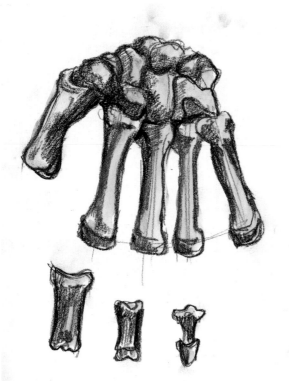

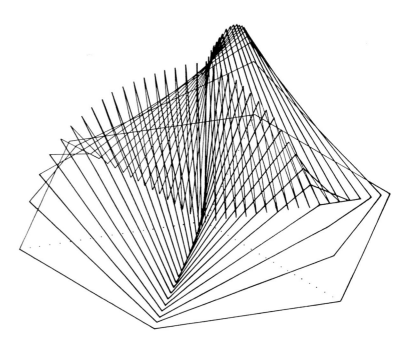

This page: Anatomical study of human hand by Calatrava; geometrical drawing of folding structure. Opposite: Unfolding doors, Ernsting Warehouse, Coesfeld-Lette

transformation. Aspects of strength of materials were then abstracted with the tacit assumption that the problem of materials was to be solved independently at a later stage when the chosen scheme was to be constructed.

The way frames can fold is constrained by joint mechanisms allowing the rigid bodies connected at the pivots by means of joints, pins, or similar devices that allow them some degree of freedom of movement. Once these initial definitions are applied to the simple case of the rhombus, the basic idea of a modular system for an infinite number of frames is introduced. The study progressed, with Calatrava constructing and exploring possible cases of such structures by augmenting step-by-step the number of their elements, then proceeding with polyhedra and spherical frames. One could conceivably expand this repertory of constructs without end, adding to the number of their elements and relationships

to develop myriad forms, with the implicit ideal outcome that one could ultimately construct "a complete enumeration" of all possible forms.

As stated earlier, the theory of transformation recruited by Calatrava employed mechanical devices called linkages, which behave like folding structures. Being interconnected, any motion set off at one point of the linkage is propagated through the rest of the device. For this reason linkages are used to transmit power. In addition, as these points travel along prescribed paths they trace lines, straight or curved. For this reason they are also employed as instruments for drawing straight or curved lines, taking advantage of the paths traveled by points of the linkage when it is set in motion. Almost everybody knows a most elementary linkage used as a drawing instrument: the tracing compass. More complex devices can be used to draw more complex curves: cycloids, epicycloids, cardi-

oids, parabolas, or hyperbolas. More intricate linkages can trace surfaces in three dimensions, such as a surface called a hyperbolic paraboloid. This was the device that generated the revered shapes created by Gaudí. And like Gaudí, what Calatrava developed through the thesis was a storehouse of instruments, a method through which a family of forms and ultimately an "endless" number of individual shapes could be born.

With any given example of a folding structure solved, one could imagine a setting in which it can be applied. Subsequently one can conclude that since the system could generate, in theory, all possible folding structures, one could find the appropriate folding structure inside the "thesaurus" of all possible folding polyhedra that Calatrava's mechanism had generated. Given this thesaurus—or what mathematicians call a systematic enumeration of possible alternative

The human body as
a folding structure
by Calatrava

solutions constructed by exhaustively combining their constitutive elements in anticipation of future building scenarios—one could imagine going step-by-step through the entire inventory of schemes of folding frames searching for the scheme that fit best.

The same can be argued about Calatrava's second objective: to represent and generate complex and novel kinds of curved surfaces. As we have already mentioned, the above repertory of foldable structures can be seen as a kit of instruments—a special kind of compass system—able to track down and describe a very large number of complex curved surfaces. One can see, therefore, the thesaurus of folding structures being translated into a thesaurus of compasses capable of generating a systematic enumeration of a very large number, if not the complete set, of possible curved surfaces, once more in anticipation of structures to come. In

both cases, the "Calatrava thesaurus" suggested that creative design was a process of discovery rather than invention.

Although Calatrava's analytical research provided in reality an incomplete enumeration, only a microcosm of folding structures or compasses and curves, *On the Foldability of Space Frames* reveals one of the basic mechanisms through which Calatrava prepared himself as a creative designer. One can argue that the captivating configuration of the unfolding doors of the Ernsting Warehouse in Germany would have been conceived with much greater difficulty without the analytical work Calatrava invested in his dissertation on the foldability of space frames and the cache of possible solutions lined up if and when needed. The same can be argued about the structural, architectural, engineering, or sculptural projects that followed—remarkably novel, varied, and fit designs produced in a

short time. Calatrava's analytical study was carried out in deliberate preparation for his subsequent creative work, part of his lifelong "patient research," as Le Corbusier once put it.

If the investment in analysis by Calatrava was so productive, a question emerges: Would more work in this direction, a longer, more complete thesaurus, have made him a more creative designer? The answer is negative. Beyond a certain point, a very rich thesaurus becomes a labyrinth, an endless search among endless possibilities with costs that far exceed the benefits of its support. Therefore Calatrava provided a surprising, almost contradictory, alternative to analysis: analogy, by which a new form to respond to a new question can be conceived by recalling, or rather jumping quickly to a precedent, one that appears to partially match the new demands. Such reference to precedent is evident in Calatrava's sketches where the human body

resembles a folding structure, and in the way its different postures offer a variety of configurations. The sketches that fill an endless series of notebooks are Calatrava's other kind of "patient research," this time involving vision and creativity rather than counting and computation. One can argue once more that it would have been very difficult to conceive the enchanting movement of the roof of the Milwaukee Art Museum without recourse by analogy to the figures of flying birds or the Nike statues of classical antiquity.

All humans are endowed with these two contradictory, complementary intelligences, *analysis* and *analogy* but few cultivate them to further develop their potential through "patient research." Even fewer are those who are able to synthesize the division of intellectual labor between the two intelligences to create a well-tempered instrument of design as Calatrava has done.[5]

Studies of the human
body in folding positions
by Calatrava

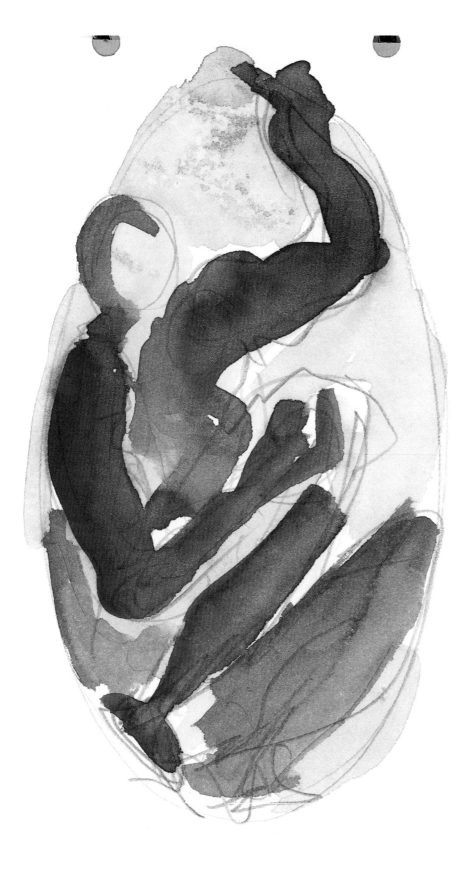

Studies of the human
body by Calatrava

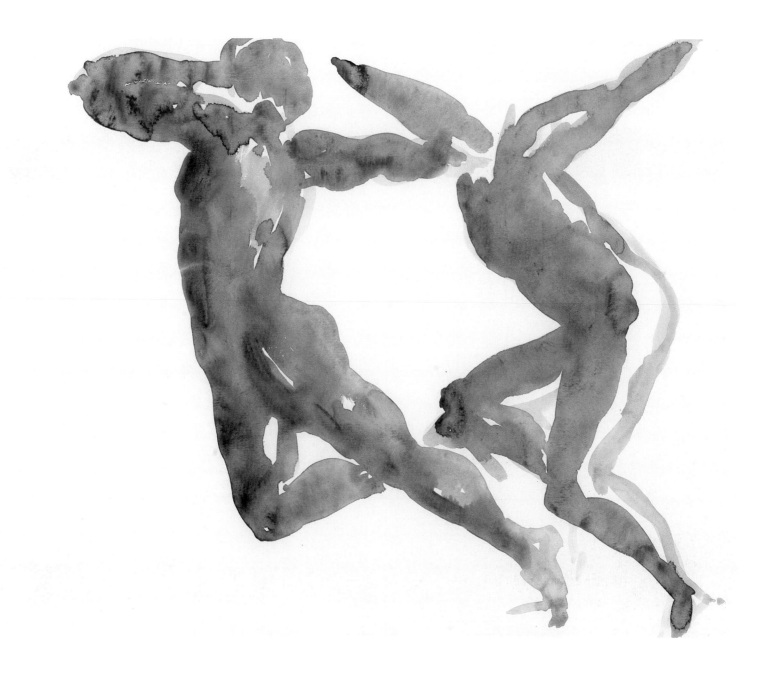

This page: Pages from one of Calatrava's notebooks. Opposite: Milwaukee Art Museum

Chapter 2 | Pregnant Moments, Nascent Structures

While still an engineering student, before the completion of his doctoral dissertation, *On the Foldability of Space Frames*, in 1981, Calatrava designed a series of bridges that anticipate the direction of his future explorations. In his early studies for a cable-stayed bridge Calatrava focused on the articulation and profiling of the joint between vertical and horizontal elements. The vertical support columns are split into a Y shape to receive the horizontal hanging deck, appearing like a vigorous man holding from his raised arms a plank suspended by ropes. At the same time the horizontal road deck thrusts between the two standing split parts of the suspending columns and over the lower standing trunk. This juxtaposition of robust and dynamic elements generates an expressive representation of movement. A similar dynamic is at work in the relationship between horizontal deck and vertical column in the cable-stayed Acleta Alpine Motor Bridge, for Disentis, in Switzerland (1979). In addition, the articulation of the joint attempts to optimize the use of materials and produces an effect of lightness and elegance. In both projects the complexity of the configuration results from a clear effort to divide labor between differentiated structural members, assigning to each a specialized task: to work in compression or in tension, in suspension or as supports, and, as a result of this division, to minimize material resources and maximize performance.

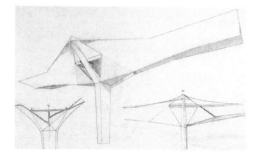

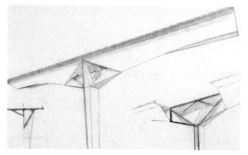

Studies for cable-stayed bridge

Almost simultaneous with the completion of his dissertation and the establishment of his practice as architect and engineer, Calatrava started designing a small number of projects. One of his very first illustrates a direct connection with the theme of his dissertation: folding. The roof for the IBA Squash Hall in Berlin was intended to be placed on top of a project by architects Fabio Reinhardt and Bruno Reichlin. Unlike the previous two bridges, the roofing looks elementary, without any special articulation of joints and profiles of the structural members. But a new concern appears to emerge: some of the parts of the structure move. The movement itself is simple, as the roof has to open and close, and to accomplish this Calatrava designed the sloping sides of the roof to move up and down. The form of the structure was emblematic rather than technical, an icon of movement into structure. It resembled a flying machine, a bird as conceived by Leonardo, a system of vertical and horizontal elements, compression and tension members connected by joints and strings. Seemingly more a gadget or a toy than part of a building, this early Calatrava artifact was a personal manifesto of what architecture could be: innovative, optimistic, rational, and playful. Retrospectively, it has a special importance in the context of the overwhelmingly formalist, nostalgic, and eclectic mood of the architecture at that time. It was also an individual declaration announcing Calatrava's intellectual quest and reputation as expert problem solver, engineer-dreamworker, architect-sculptor, and thinker-toymaker.

Moving on from the two first bridges, Calatrava appears to follow two strategies: division of mechanical labor between the various components of a structure, resulting in the articulation of individual elements; and distribution of material within each element, resulting in an elaboration of the profile of the structural elements. The two strategies collaborate towards

Model of roof structure

the achievement of an outermost limit, an "optimal" design, minimizing the consumption of resources while maximizing performance. Allowing the design to fall short of this standard leads to inefficiency. Pushing it too far leads to collapse. To put it more technically, if a certain variable in design exceeds the "critical point," the interatomic bonds, the ties between atoms of a structural member, will be broken, and the structure will fly in all directions at once. In the projects that follow, Calatrava's efforts to achieve this "optimal" state operate on a technical level while at the same time attempting to achieve a form that represents how the structure

stands. He tries to "explain" to the viewer the mechanical workings of the structure, thus the overarticulation and elaboration of the structure here: by looking at the object one can envision the operations of nature.

This idea also appears in the lightweight industrial shed for Jakem, a steel construction company, in Münchwilen, Switzerland, which Calatrava began designing in 1983, a seminal year in his life. The construction of the shed was finished by 1984. Initially, Calatrava came in contact with Jakem in 1981, the year he received his doctorate degree, to inspect the company's products for a wide-span girder system for the

Züspa Exhibition Hall competition in Zurich. When Jakem commissioned him to design a shed structure, Calatrava seized the opportunity to investigate more generally roof systems, and to experiment and test his ideas under real conditions. Instead of a flat roof, a lighter, slender, triangulated girder system was proposed. Each girder is composed of a pair of identical, two-dimensional bowstring trusses: a curved upper and a straight bottom stringer joined by struts and stiffened by corrugated sheet forming a triangulated framework. The system proved to be efficient and was patented to serve as a departure point for later projects.

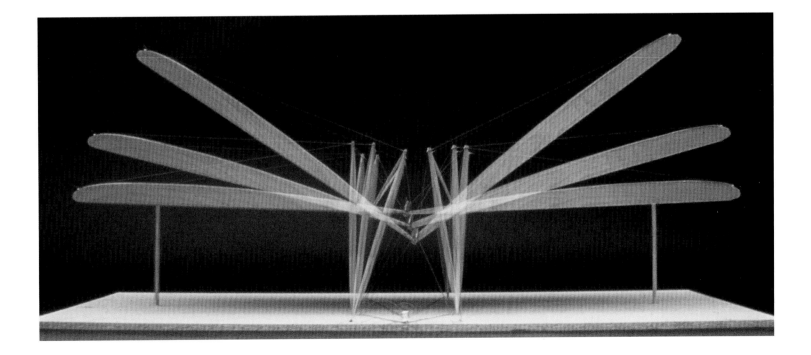

A more important project indicative of Calatrava's new path was the Ernsting Warehouse, in Coesfeld-Lette, Germany, also commissioned in 1983 and completed in 1985. Calatrava was able to experiment with many new ideas despite the fact that he was a partner in collaboration with two other architects, Fabio Reinhardt and Bruno Reichlin, for a very limited assignment. The commission called for the design of aluminum cladding for an existing structure, a large concrete frame with masonry infill designed by Gerzi, a firm specializing in buildings for the textile industry. But the client, a casual-wear retailer, hoped that the cladding would also provide a unique, identifiable icon for the firm.

Given the fact that the structure and plan of the building were already determined by the design of Gerzi, the task was to conceive an image based on the architecture of the skin. The form of the building was a freestanding, plain orthogonal prism. To this severe, rigid body Calatrava infused lightness and grace, attempting for the first time to translate the corpus of theoretical knowledge developed in his dissertation into a design strategy beyond optimization and representation of the critical moment. With this project Calatrava began to develop a poetics of movement, which becomes more manifest in the bridge projects he designs two years later.

Movement is apparent in the enclosure of the Ernsting Warehouse, but it is more pictorial than structural. Interestingly the project depicts movement while preserving the basic static simplicity of the prismatic rectilinear form of the volume designed by Gerzi. Even more interesting is that within the framework of Gerzi's volume, or rather around it, Calatrava decided to adopt a formal composition that adheres to the spatial canon of the ancient Greek classical temple. The work reminds one of Alberti surrounding the old structure of the Tempio Malatestiano with a classical dress. As a building rethinking the classical canon setting it in the horizon of our times, the building achieves the same level of success as the twentieth-century masterpieces of modern neoclassicism by Le Corbusier and Mies.

However, in contrast to Le Corbusier and Mies's schemes, where the classical canon was applied to the buildings' structural elements, Calatrava's design for the Ernsting Warehouse applied it on the enclosing material, the skin or dress. The draping, horizontal cascading of the facade recalls the visual effect of the colonnade of the temples of antiquity. As the convex-concave sequences of the grooves and shafts of the classical Doric columns in a temple wave rhythmically in the sun, so the 102 meters of corrugated aluminum cladding material ripple in the southern light; as the columns of a Doric temple feature no base, so the cladding at the concrete

View of doors folded open

ground plane without a termination. And as in the classical temples, the overall composition of the facade follows a tripartite schema of top termination, main body, and base divisions, while the corners of the building are accentuated.

The three large service entrances on the flat facade of the building, however, do not fit in this schema. They are embedded in the volume like special bas-relief episodes from a classical building but standing outside the classical canon. The door elements are made out of aligned, vertical aluminum slats articulated in a kneelike manner to move up and down; they are hinged along a curved line and connected at their lower points to a horizontal frame, which can be raised or lowered. When the frame is raised, opening the doors by means of a hidden mechanism, the vertical slats leave the plane of the facade and protrude forward, while the vertical slats fold like the drapes of an ancient Greek tunic over a bent knee. The effect is stressed due to the differentiated triple-jointing of each U-shaped, extruded profile through which they assume the shape of a graceful cantilevered roof. Functionally, the extruded profile provides a kind of protective canopy over the entrance. The swooping line of the canopy is generated by the gradual and uniform change of the position of the series of slats: lower at the sides, higher toward the center—a simple, functional, and wholly original solution (patented later by Calatrava).

Very few contemporary buildings exploit to such an extent the potential of enveloping skin and folding. Calatrava's fluttering curtain wall is a comment on Gottfried Semper's claim that the principle of dressing, *Bekleidung*, rather than structure or plan, is the true source of architecture.[1] And of course one should not forget that Ernsting is itself a textile firm.

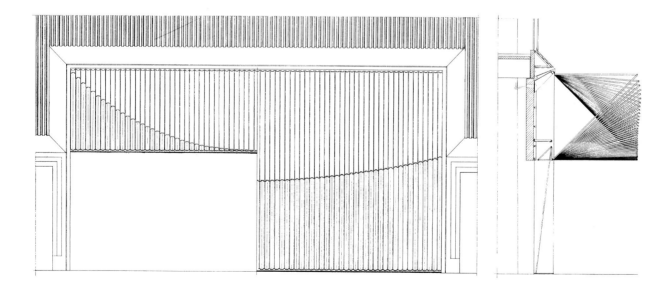

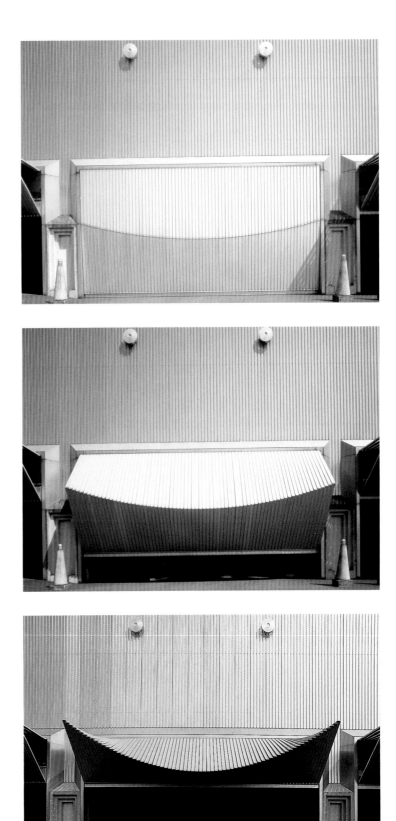

This page: Folding doors
in operation. Opposite:
Drawings of folding
door mechanism

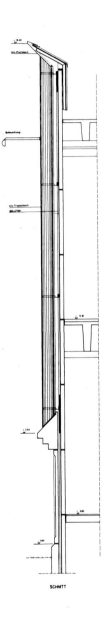

SCHNITT

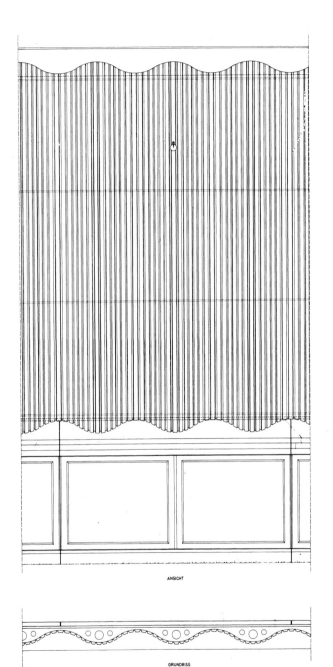

ANSICHT

GRUNDRISS

This page: Construction
drawings of wall. Oppo-
site: View of south wall

Stadelhofen Railway Station Zurich, Switzerland

In 1983 Calatrava, with Arnold Amsler and Werner Ruegger, participated in a competition to design the Stadelhofen Railway Station in Zurich for the suburban rail network—the first rapid transit system to be built in Switzerland. The entry was awarded the first prize and the commission. The project, by far the most challenging of Calatrava's career up to that moment, was the first complete expression of his poetics of movement. By definition the program of the project was driven by the need to accommodate the circulation of vehicles and people. Although stations were a major theme for architects during the 1950s, since the mid-1960s architectural interest in them declined, and functionality soon dominated cultural considerations. Calatrava's project, as well as other subsequent projects for stations and terminals, helped reverse this neg-

ative trend. They are architectural infrastructure works that refer to the romance of travel at the turn of the twentieth century with a fusion of structure and movement.

The site is a dense urban area of Zurich, between Stadelhofen Square and the Hohenpromenade hill (once a bastion of the old city's fortifications). Calatrava's intention was to disrupt the urban fabric and the landscape of the nearby hill, and he proposed an open platform while respecting the slope of the terrain. The hill is retained by a concrete boxbeam with a convex soffit, supported by an anchored, piled wall at the rear and a series of triple-point, slanting, and tapering columns at the front. The structure consists of a continuous 270-meter section, following the gentle curve of the tracks under the hill. Above the boxbeam, running its full length, is a promenade,

enhanced by a cable trellis to create a light green "canopy." From this promenade travelers reach the platforms via stairs and an elevator, or cross over bridges that span the tracks to the lower side.

Covering the opposite side of the tracks is a cantilevered roof system in which winged columns hoist up a torsion tube attached to steel flange purloins. Two steel awnings adjacent to the station protect travelers entering the subterranean shopping center and close off the entry in the evening. A road bridge follows the gradient of the hill, while two pedestrian bridges are supported by a triangulated structure. Stairs and escalators flanking the original station building increase accessibility, and underground connect to create a subterranean shopping center. The exposed concrete ceiling is one continuous, undulating surface. Daylight filters

This page: Site plan.
Opposite: View from platforms

down through prefabricated glass-brick elements laid in the platforms to illuminate the shop fronts. Once more Calatrava designed the station as a total artifact including the supports for the overhead power-cable brackets for the trains.

Calatrava has referred to the scheme as "design by section," which was a rather contrary statement at a moment when abstract graphics and concern with the facade dominated architecture. Calatrava's section drawings show multiple circulation systems involving the differentiation and articulation of several kinds of transportation modes. The scheme is indeed a three-dimensional, well-packed, well-woven arrangement of tightly interlocked, superposed routes of different scales, qualities of movement, and points of transition. It also accommodates different flow types: the fast regular flow of trains along the tracks cutting through the ground

level; the hasty pedestrian flow entering and leaving the vehicles along the platforms, approaching and leaving the station, ascending and descending its three levels, mingling or walking through the shopping center, which extends beneath the tracks to additionally serve as an underpass; and the flow of pedestrians crossing above the tracks over three steel bridges, transversing both hillside and plain to access the existing road system. There is a slow, leisurely flow of Baudelairian flaneurs, where pedestrians can stroll up and down the hill, along the promenade, over the pedestrian bridge, through the stairs and escalators to the shopping area and then out to the street. There is also the penetrating flow of light cascading down to the shopping center through the glass and metal roof and the glass blocks of the sidewalks, as well as the "organic" flow of light running through the branches and stems of the

vines spreading over the steel pergola that sweeps back from the promenade's edge toward the hill.

And one must not forget the flow of forces within and through the members of the structure channeled down to the ground via the intricate configurations of the structure: the various materials such as steel and reinforced concrete, and structural elements such as columns, beams, cantilevers, platforms, and supporting walls. Structures appear to be, but are never, at rest. And the more that is known about their behavior, the more one realizes how indispensable movement is in them. Although apparently immobile, under closer scrutiny all structures, both artificial and natural, prove to be in a state of constant motion. Buildings, bridges, sculpture, trees, and even mountains are all constantly deformed, flexed, stretched, and squeezed. They slide and roll. They bend and bow. They sway, tremble, and

Sketch of section,
by Calatrava

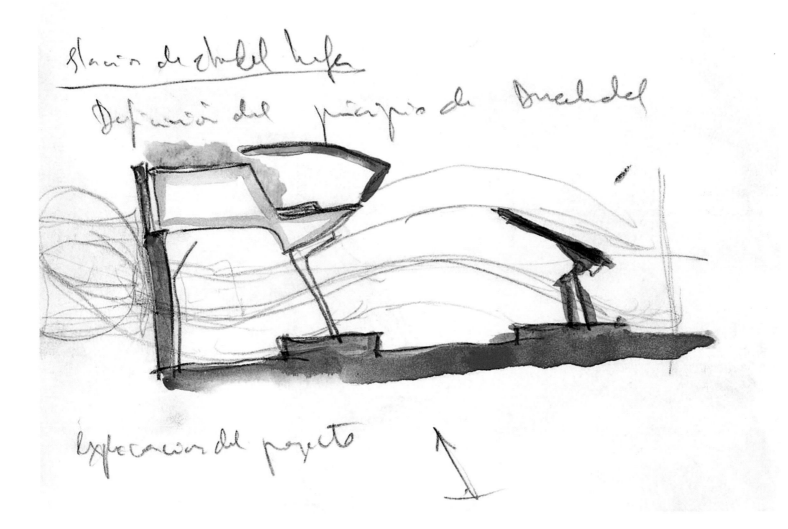

shudder. Most of the time such movement is imperceptible and momentary, leaving the overall stability and permanence of the body of the structure undisturbed.

This is the movement, however, that Calatrava invites the viewer to envision in the structure's form through the specific articulation of members and the geometrical elaboration of their profile. For example, the columns of Stadel-hofen branch into a Y-shaped configuration to improve their structural performance. But a peculiar structural motif also emerges: an S, zigzag, palindrome figure repeated through several structural elements. What occurs here is a structure configured so that its elements seem to take apart the whole while also encountering an opposing force, so that taken together the various forces contribute to create a balanced ensemble. This is a highly intelligent strategy to achieve a structure of optimal efficiency and effectiveness. It is also a way of demonstrating more expressively the invisible workings of material and form that make an object stand. The S configuration will return almost obsessively in Calatrava's projects as a kind of trademark figure, but more importantly as a way to signify in his later work cognitive and moral concerns.

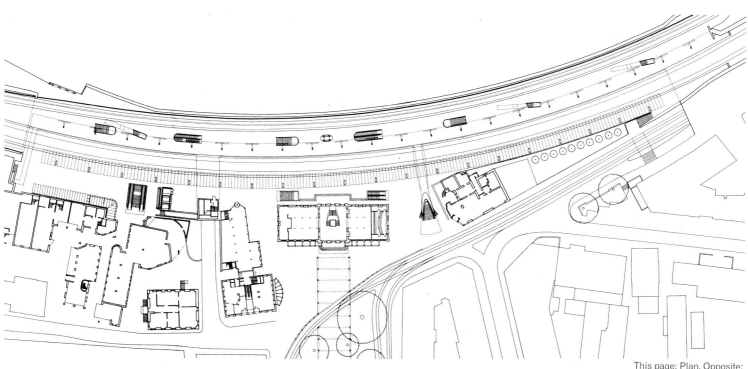

This page: Plan. Opposite: View of platform with cantilevered roof system. Overleaf: View showing the two levels above ground

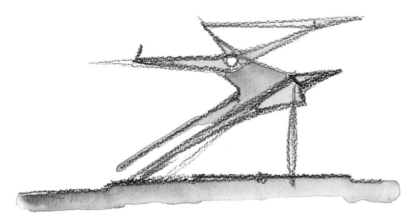

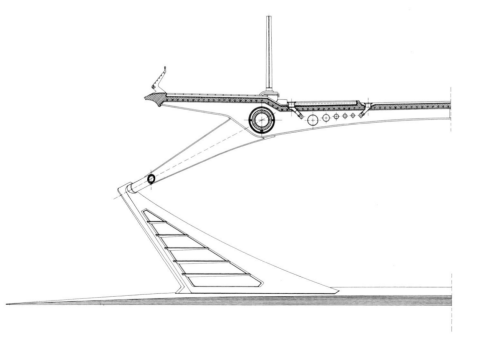

This page: Drawing
by Calatrava (above);
construction drawing of
Kronprinzen footbridge
(below). Opposite page:
Section through existing
building (above); section
through pedestrian
bridge (below)

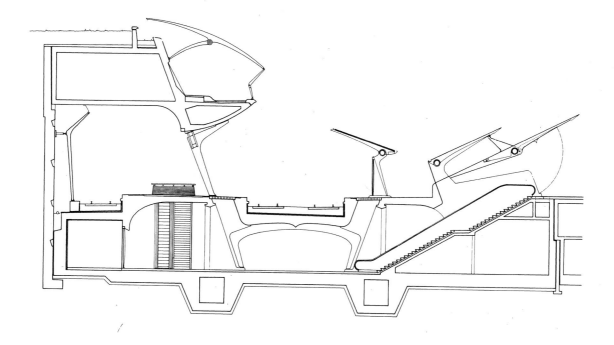

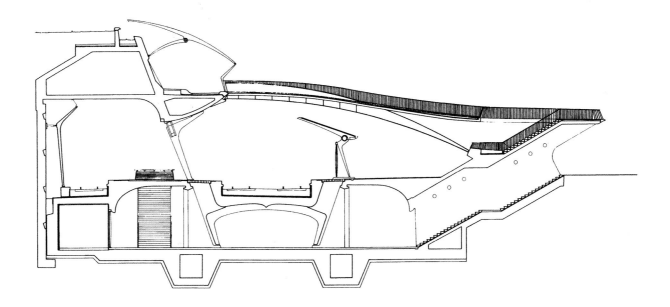

This page: Promenade
with canopy. Opposite:
Construction drawing
of canopy

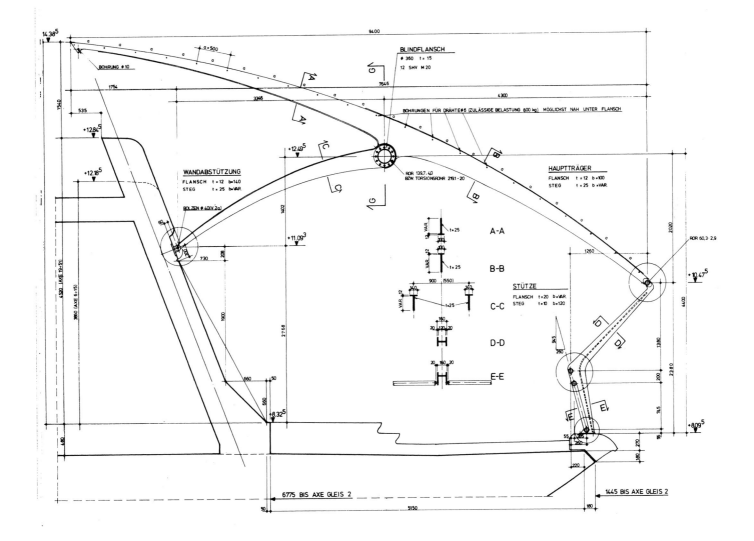

Two views of platform
under the hill

Two views of under-
ground passage

Canopies and pergolas comprised many of Calatrava's early commissions, but the same time it is clear that they are a theme that fascinates him. The Thalberg House balcony extension in Zurich (1983), one of his first professional assignments, includes a carefully designed canopy, as does the PTT Postal Center in Lucerne (1983–85) and the St. Fiden Bus Shelter in St. Gallen (1983–85). Perhaps the reason for this fascination is the projects' folding potential, real or virtual, again implying movement as the winglike canopies reach away from the main volume. Similarly, the canopy is the dominant element as one approaches the Wohlen High School, Wohlen, Switzerland. Burkhard, Meyer & Steiger—the architects who had won the local competition to build the new and expanded Wohlen High School—asked Calatrava to submit proposals for the roofing of four key public spaces in the project. For each of these Calatrava used a different system of construction.

Calatrava designed the canopy to be supported by a steel, tubular arch that runs obliquely along the surface of the glazed facade. Spanning 20 meters, this arched spine is the point of attachment for a series of tapering profiles that make up the ribs supporting the two glazed, dihe-

dral surfaces that form the sections of two intersecting cones. In plan, the outer edges of these surfaces are parallel, with the arch running diagonally across their combined rhomboid shape, a structural spatial motif to which Calatrava will return repeatedly in the future.

For the irregularly shaped entrance hall, Calatrava provided a circular opening in the roof. A series of radial, repeating timber units fills the open circle and rests on a steel tension ring at its edge. Each petal-like segment is gracefully cut away, and loads are carried to the central compression ring through laminated and turned pine spindles set in steel sleeves. The units are 5.4 meters in length on their lower sides, and the pattern is repeated twenty times to create a design that invokes the form of a flower over an opening 11.4 meters in diameter. The diameter of the glazed roof lantern is 2 meters.

The roof of the library, which is located off the lobby, consists of four thin, reinforced planes that meet to create a complex shape reminiscent of an open book. A single, strengthened, steel column 4 meters high is placed at the intersection of the four vaults that make up the space, supporting the entire weight of the roof

while also serving as the downspout for rainwater. The shape of the shell allows daylight to enter the space below. Discreetly placed steel spindles stabilize the cast in situ roof.

The concrete columns of the assembly hall are cast in two bonded halves and are designed to directly absorb the loads transmitted by the roof structure. They face each other as a mirror image across the vault of the auditorium. The assembly hall also functions as a large music room with modern electronics studio. At 16 by 28 meters, it is roofed by five precisely prefabricated three-pin parabolic arches that span 8 meters.

The arches create a deep triangulated section. Individual rough-cut, untreated pine battens—organized in a radial pattern fanning upward from a theoretical midpoint below the floor surface—form the braces between the laminated lower member and the shallower parabola of the upper members. The upper members are joined by acoustically treated horizontal board. The arches bear the full weight of the barrel roof, thus relieving the walls and enabling the skylight to run the full length of the roof's edge. Concrete, timber, steel, and glass are employed to bring in, reflect, and control light.

Entrance canopy

This page: Roof lantern
in entrance hall. Oppo-
site: View of the library

View of assembly hall

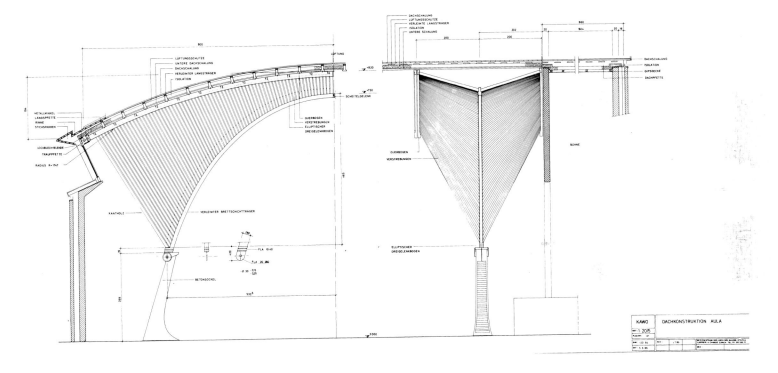

Construction drawing
of structure

This page: Detail of
structure. Opposite:
Roof of assembly hall

The canopy-portico is the dominant theme in the Lucerne Station Hall. In 1983, SBB, the Swiss rail system, commissioned Calatrava to produce a design for the entrance hall and portico of its new station in Lucerne, originally built in 1896 to plans by Jean Béguin and Hubert Stier and reworked by Hans Auer, and destroyed by fire in 1971. Calatrava conceived the lightweight glazed structure as a distinctive and totally independent volume extending the length of the station facade. With a portico that responds to the old town, the structure maintains proportions drawn from the neighboring neoclassical buildings. The roof of the portico is cantilevered from sixteen prefabricated concrete columns, each 14 meters high, that line the 109-meter facade, braced by a row of interconnected steel tension-spindles. In the new portico entrance Calatrava used the same columnar motif as in the Stadel-hofen Station, as well as the strategy of optimizing structure through differentiation and profiling of the most distinguished element of the project, in this case the portico. Other strategies are repeated as well: the same formal balancing act, the same specialized devices to act in compression and tension to keep the structure stable, the same effect of apparent movement throughout the profile. But the motifs are carried here to a gigantic scale, as in a Renaissance colonnade. The sixteen monumental, precast concrete columns stand as testaments to the complex movement within and around the sub-level concourse area it envelops.

This page: Interior of hall from above. Opposite: View of station and its concrete portico. Overleaf: The transparent portico facade

The strategy of developing highly articulated and profiled structural members of construction is accentuated in the roof for the Bärenmatte Community Center, Suhr, Switzerland. The structure became even more intricate and complex because constraints related to the flow of light as well as the flow of forces informed the structure's configuration. Initially the town council of Suhr needed a hall for concerts and other cultural and community events and asked Cala-

trava, in association with Hertig and Partners, to develop a spatial concept fitting the dimensions of the hall, for which the stage and foyer had already been finalized. Within these tight constraints, typical of most projects Calatrava undertook at the beginning of his career, he proposed a roof spanning the entire interior space, pitched and staggered for efficiency, and for contextual reasons combining a configuration that incorporates a raised ridge with skylights.

The roof is supported by a series of three-pin, tied arches, which are composed of tapering, curved box-girders of welded steel plate, triangulated at their outer ends and achieving a flat, prismatic section of 3 meters at their uppermost points beneath the ridge. The intriguing complexity of the roof structure's form resulted from the intelligent differentiation of its components much like organs, operating in a specialized manner to respond to static and lighting constraints.

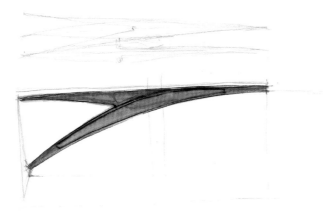

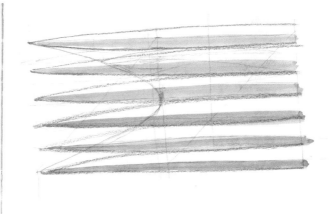

Preliminary sketches
by Calatrava

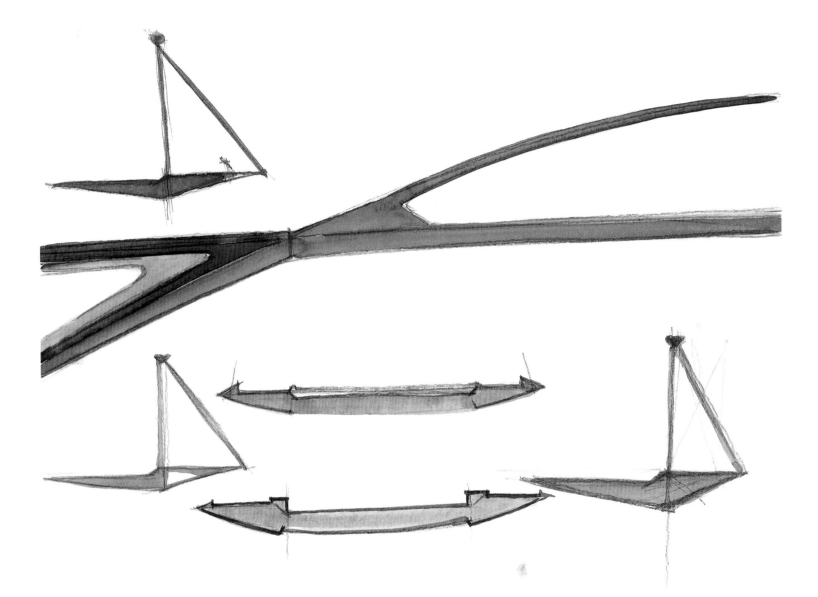

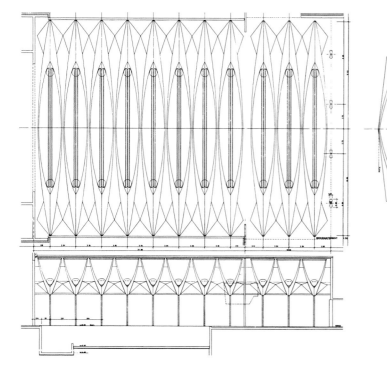

This page: View of hall
(above); plan and
sections of hall (below).
Opposite: Detail of
light fixtures and
tension cables

Though the Caballeros Footbridge, Lerida, Spain, was never constructed, it played however a major role in the development of Calatrava's ideas because it was here that the scheme of a single-pier suspension bridge emerged. The bridge was conceived as an extension of the Calle des Caballeros, which ends at the city's medieval walls, to connect the old urban core with the woods and fields on the other side of the Segre River. The choice of a single-pier scheme grounded on the town side was dictated by the unstable nature of the terrain on the wooded side. Thus on the higher bank of the river a single steel pylon was cantilevered from a reinforced concrete support set on a pile foundation. The light steel and aluminum walkway spans 140 meters and is suspended over the river by cable stays hung from the pylon.

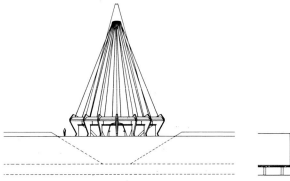
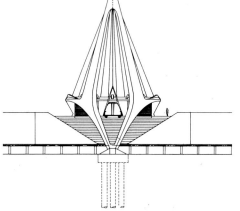

This page: Elevations of pylon from town side and from country side with section through walkway. Opposite: Model

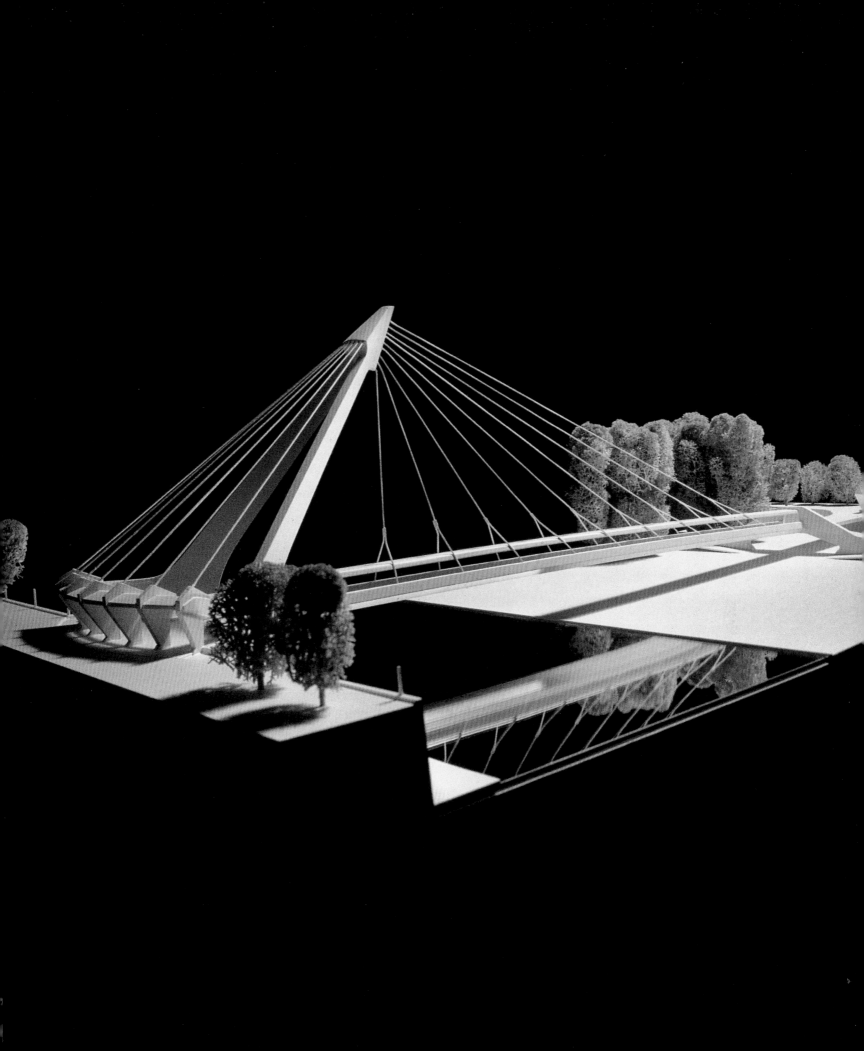

Bach de Roda Bridge Barcelona, Spain

As the requirements of Calatrava's commissions began to increase in complexity—largely due to stringent demands to integrate more types of movement in the same component of a project—Calatrava began to develop increasingly sophisticated strategies to allow different flows to coincide and cooperate within the structure. As a result, the projects appear simpler and richer. The stepped entrance to the footpath of the 128-meter-long Bach de Roda Bridge, Barcelona, Spain, demonstrates the various movements of pedestrian, car, and train into a nexus of conduits: the ascending stair and ascending arch join to form a multifunctional container within which the integrity of each flow is equally preserved. Further on, the flow of pedestrian movement intercepts the flow of forces, cutting through the middle of the concrete arch support at exactly the point where the resulting void does not weaken the structure; in other words, where the presence of material is redundant. Similarly, the channel for lighting is embedded in the channel for the handrail, and follows the same rules of differentiation between flows, articulation of channels, and spatial cooperation between channels.

Calatrava was given the opportunity to develop these ideas by Barcelona's planning authority, which commissioned the bridge to connect the area of Sant Andrea in the north to San Marti in the south, on the fringes of the Cerda town plan. This initiative, which was part of a scheme to revitalize two impoverished areas of the city, also included the construction of a new railway station close by. The wide, flat embankments of the railway were to be transformed into a continuation of the Parc de la Clot, thus creating one of the most expansive green areas in the city. The bridge serves both automotive traffic and pedestrians and also connects the two sides of a major rail link. The main steel arches, which flank the roadway, are placed directly at the edge of the traffic lanes and are supported by streamlined reinforced concrete pylons. Attenuated abutments support the secondary, steel-stiffening arches canted against the main arches. Here the strategy of cooperation through competition appears in the leaning arches, which eliminate the need for a truss between the main arches. The solution rethinks the more traditional approach to arch buckling, i.e., bracing arch pairs via interconnecting trusses, by placing secondary arches of equal height adjacent to the main arches, leaning them inward, and connecting them by fins to brace both arches against buckling.

Responding to the contextual needs, Calatrava's scheme made the bridge visible from a distance so that it became a recognizable and memorable landmark against the urban landscape. The bridge becomes a true instrument of universal accessibility. Its stairs provide access to parks on either side, visually continuing the direction of the supporting abutments. The pedestrian areas of the bridge are widened into the form of a bow between each pair of steel arches within a space defined by the suspension cables to create two new suspended urban balconies. Rather than operating as an instrument of one-dimensional utility, the Bach de Roda Bridge represents the first of Calatrava's technologically innovative infrastructure projects to restore connections to and interactions with the surrounding community.

Opposite: Parallel flows of vehicles and pedestrians. Overleaf: View showing main and secondary arches

The bridge above
rail tracks

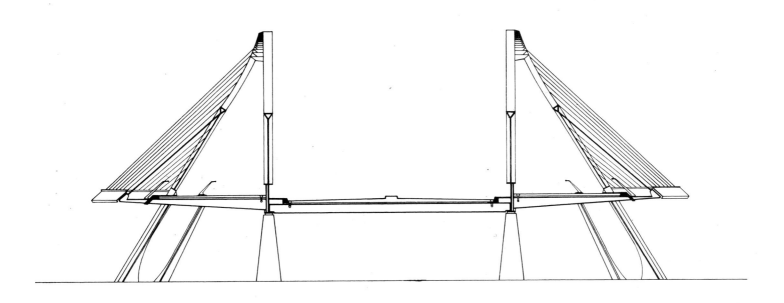

Cross section and
side elevation

In spite of his introduction to large-scale engineering projects, Calatrava did not lose interest in designing domestic-scale structures. His commitment to design remained as universal as the mechanisms of creativity in general. The Tabourettli Theater, Basel, Switzerland, was a modest project that involved introducing a new theater space into a thirteenth-century building, a task which Calatrava carried out with fastidious attention to the smallest detail. The structure was a feat for its time, but it has required major changes to keep it intact while also adapting it to the changing demands of a working theater. Calatrava's minimal intervention was effective and saved the building without changing its character leaving freedom to insert his own work. A true *Gesamtkunstwerk*, it included a new acoustic ceiling; new window shutters, which fold idiosyncratically upward; a lobby featuring a folding octagonal box containing bar, light fittings, and furniture; and a staircase that floats above the floor and acts as a trestle to carry weight away from the foundation to a centrally located basement support. Most evident in the project is the articulation of the spanning structure. Like organic tissue, Calatrava's design gradually differentiates and specializes, discriminating between constraints of compression, tension, and torsion to optimize material performance.

The array of vibrant projects produced during the early years of Calatrava's practice have a clear and direct relationship to the pages of his dissertation devoted to the analysis of foldability and movement of structures. However, this is only one source of the stream of creative activity, one half of Calatrava's poetics of movement. The other source emerges from the endless pages of Calatrava's notebooks.

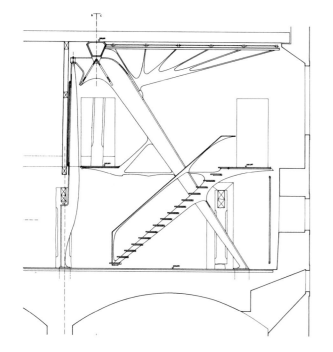

This page: Section through staircase. Opposite: View of stairway looking down

Chapter 3 | Metamorphoses and Heuristic Dreams

Confronted with the huge corpus of drawings contained in Calatrava's notebooks, one is prompted to ask a question analogous to that brought up by his dissertation: Why would an engineer spend so much time producing sketchbooks filled with figures of human bodies and dancers, doves, fish, and other animals, plants, and everyday objects? But upon investigation the sketches in the notebooks emerge as a "second source" of the stream of creative design that characterizes Calatrava's development, the "other half" of the poetics of movement through which Calatrava has conceived his inventive projects.

There are hundreds of notebooks, each one often containing more than a hundred drawings by Calatrava. As documents, the notebooks are the "hot," Dionysian counterpart to the "cold," Apollonian dissertation. To use a familiar metaphor, the dissertation was committed to the analysis of structures while the notebooks are dedicated to the analogy between figures. Taken together, the dissertation and the notebooks provide a key to understanding the complementarity between analysis and analogy in Calatrava's work and to the inventiveness of his design. Working together, analysis and analogy offer a well-tempered feedback system that has done much to enhance Calatrava's robustness as a creator.

The line of thought driving the dissertation was stern, circumscribed, and targeted. By contrast, the visions on display in the pages of the notebooks fly, fluctuate, and fuse with each other: the figure of a man with open arms becomes an open book and then melts to become the prow of a boat, while another human dissolves to become a bull's skull.

Such analogies, frightfully irrational as they may appear—matching objects seemingly unrelated and irrelevant to each other—are essential even for engineers and scientists to solve complex problems when analysis, enumeration, and assessment of possible solutions is impossible. In the search for things unknown, referring to known quantities may be helpful in making the unfamiliar familiar. And Calatrava endeavored to identify the form and function of many unknown things, particularly for moving structures. As the drawings in the notebooks attest, by making extensive use of analogy Calatrava could discover, transform, and reuse precedents, often from nature, to solve new problems.

Thinking by analogy, making associations with past experiences, is a common tool to cope with everyday life. Analogy is also the stuff out of which poetic metaphors are made. But it is also a powerful tool for confronting exceptional scientific and technological problems, which is

Visual analogies between a man with open arms, a book, and a boat, by Calatrava

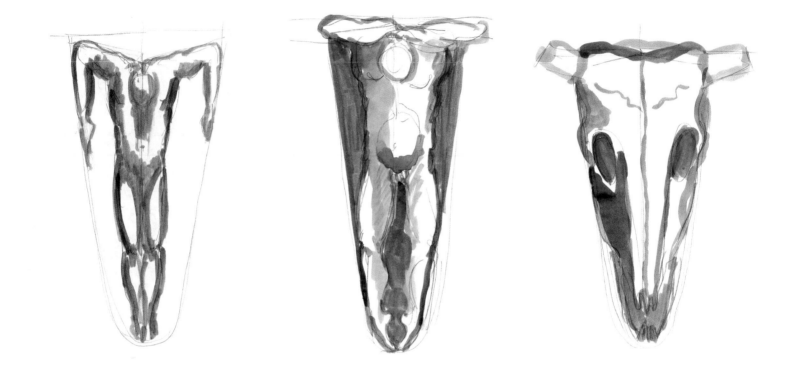

how Calatrava put it to work in his own poetics, as the notebooks reveal.[1] Using analogy as a tool, creative scientists have overcome hurdles of ignorance and achieved great breakthroughs, frequently employing the wildest associations. Such was the famous case of biochemist Friedrich August Kekulé von Stradonitz, whose vision of a snake biting its own tail led to a new model of the cyclic molecular structure of carbon in benzene, in 1865. Similarly, we know from the text and sketches in Leonardo's notebooks that when he tried to design the wing of a flying machine, an object then without precedent, he referred to the form and function of the wings of birds, bats, and "other kinds of flying insects." Leonardo returned to the problem more than once in his notebooks, with the bulk of his inquiry contained in a small booklet in Florence in 1505 as *Sul Volo degli Uccelli* (*Codex Atlanticus*), or *On the Flight of Birds.* His strategy was to couple analogy with analysis of the wings' forms, since he was convinced that they were "working according to mathematical law."[2]

Similarly, the technological-spatial problem that preoccupied Calatrava—identifying the form of moving structures for buildings—was new and required analysis, as the pages of his dissertation show. But without the use of analogy his solutions certainly would have been much more limited. The potential of analogy to access new, not yet sufficiently exploited territories of knowledge is manifested in the dissertation itself, where Calatrava drew from the mechanisms of NASA to address the question of foldability in structures. And of course the configuration and movement of the human body was the analogy used to generate what engineers call the "pre-parametric" scheme for the graceful folding doors of the Ernsting Warehouse. Calatrava himself has argued that the folding form-function of the eye was particularly important for this conception.[3]

The pages of the notebooks also contain schemes for components of buildings, bridges, or infrastructure projects that expand or contract, open or close, rise or fall, and these can be interpreted as analogies to the forms and functions of a soaring bird or a blooming flower. The Harvard biologist Richard Lewontin has used the term *recruiting* to describe the natural phenomenon of organs assuming new functions when faced with new external conditions.[4] A similar process of recruitment is employed by Calatrava in his notebooks to give shape to objects not yet

Visual analogies between a human body and a bull's skull, by Calatrava

born, such as the form of a new column or beam, or a roof structure to fulfill new programmatic requirements or contextual conditions. A prime example the recruitment of a human torso to create an abstract construction of rotated stacked cubes that later became a sculpture and subsequently led to the invention of a new form for the Malmö Turning Torso Tower in Sweden and the 80 South Street Tower in Manhattan.

Analogy is an abstract cognitive process taking place in the mind using sensory material that can be visual, acoustic, or kinesthetic. Analogical "recruiting" can be an effortless association, but it can also involve negotiation and deliberation. In this respect drawings can be of great help as the mind struggles to recall, focus, match, and test. As much as Calatrava's sketches are aesthetic objects to gaze at, their intentions are to record and reflect. They enabled him not only to disclose similarities between static shapes but also to envision resemblances between the movements carried out by objects. Thus the type of movement occurring in an object prototype could be projected to the movement performed by an object conceived sometime in the future.

As Liane Lefaivre has suggested, Calatrava's drawings bring to mind those of Leon Battista Alberti, the great Renaissance architect and theoretician who five hundred years ago wrote about his own way of designing by recombination and fusion: "I am accustomed, most of all at night, to investigate and construct in my mind some unheard-of machine for moving and carrying weights. And sometimes it has happened that . . . I have thought of things most rare and memorable. Sometimes I have designed and built wonderfully composed buildings in my mind, combining different orders and many columns with diverse capitals and unusual bases, and adding to these cornices and entablatures, conferring upon the whole a harmonious and new grace."[5]

Analogy in this case not only helps creativity by making new associations but also by liberating the designer from fixed associations and biases. This process of liberation can lack any sense of search and direction so that it is less like investigating after an end and more like wandering and dreaming. Calatrava's long hours of free associative, roaming drawing, or what Lefaivre has called "dreamwork," suggest a strong relationship with Freud's ideas on creativity. This process is also reminiscent of the great French mathematician Jules-Henri Poincaré's description of his own creative process as one of dismantling and recombining, whereby "ideas rise in crowds . . . collide . . . until pairs interlocked so to speak making a stable combination . . . the most fertile [being] those formed

Pages from Calatrava's notebooks showing human torso and torso sculpture

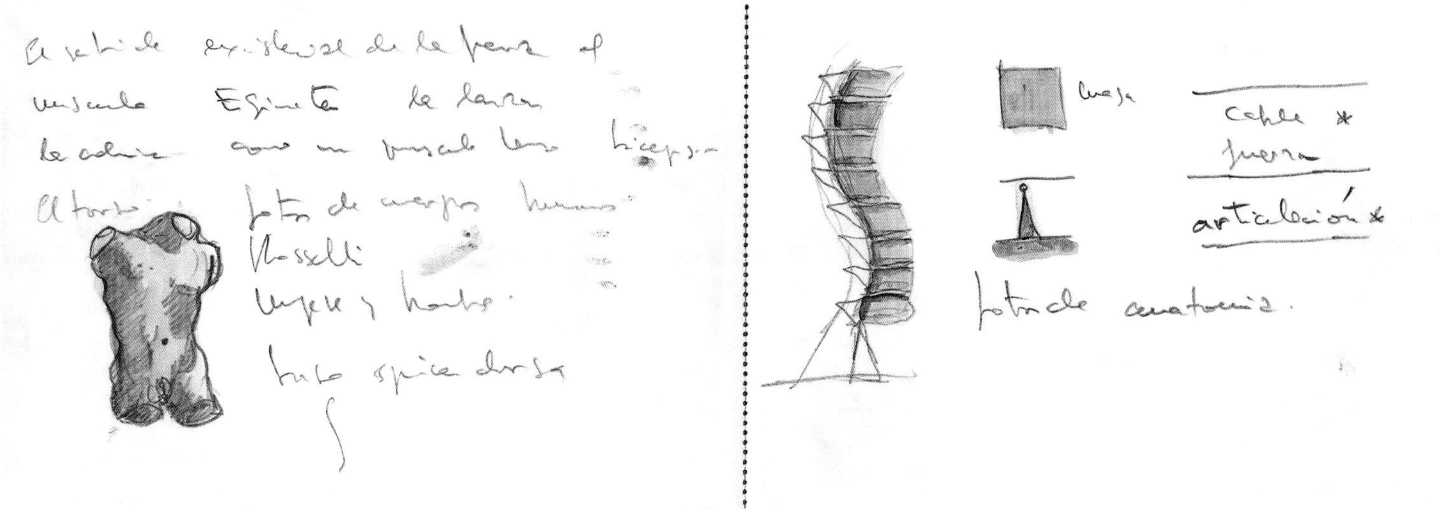
masa
cable *
fuerza
articulación *
fotos de anatomía.

of elements drawn from domains which are far apart."[6]

One should not be afraid to apply the term *surrealistic* to Calatrava's analogies, suggesting as it does the creative, critical, and liberating role played by the Surrealists in the 1930s as defined by Lewis Mumford in his 1936 review of the Surrealist show at the Museum of Modern Art in New York. According to Mumford the intellectual contribution of the Surrealists was to liberate "the willing, wishing, urging, passionate part of man's life," which had been "slighted, stifled, and even banished altogether in favor of practical routines."[7] Thus analogy enhances not only the conception of a new form but also the infusion of a new meaning in an old function. It not only assists the conception of new forms, as with the folding doors of the Ernsting Warehouse, but also helps to transform merely functional doors into a wink, a smile, a bending knee, a ris-

ing gown, an extending wing, infusing poetry and drama into the structure of the building.

In addition to drawings suggesting analogies, the notebooks contain repertories of human figures in varying postures. Obsessively produced one after the other, these series of figures do not only explore the variety of folding structures shown in chapter 1. They are derived from the transformation of an S- or zigzag-shaped human figure, similar to the "palindrome" structural motif of the columns of Stadelhofen Station, which lean to the brink of falling. Calatrava returns zealously to this motif to shape structures in several projects almost as a trademark. But there is more to the figure than a memorable emblem.

The characteristics of the motif applied in built form also appear in Calatrava's human figures, suggesting a structure whose components individually seem to act against each other, try-

ing to take it apart while also working together to create a balanced ensemble. Therefore a perusal of the figures in the drawings offers a variety of visual analogies derived from a basic motif, the S configuration. It is another kind of enumeration of structures whose equilibrium ensures that for every force that threatens to topple it there is an equally resistant force.

The S motif that dominates the work of Calatrava in all its expressions—architecture, engineering, art, and other objects—has great significance in terms of the representation of movement within the history of visual culture. As opposed to the folding structures, where movement was explicitly realized by the mechanism of the structure, here movement is implied by the form of the structure. Since antiquity artists and writers have been fascinated with the problem of representing movement. Ancient Greek sculpture evolved by gradually disengaging the

Drawing from
Calatrava's notebooks

Drawings from
Calatrava's notebooks

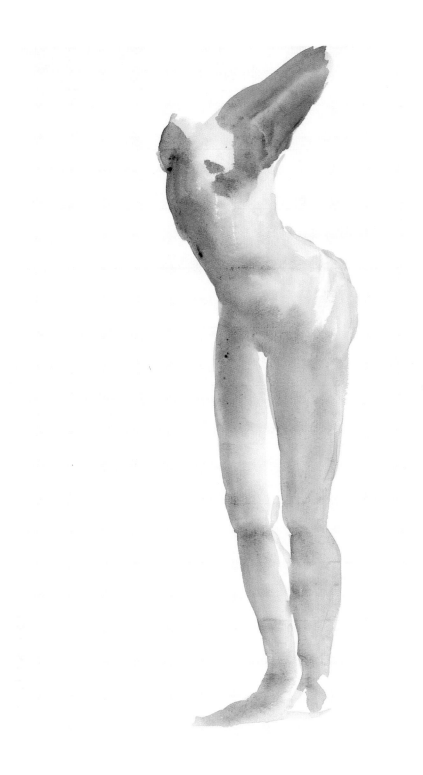

human body from the block of stone to achieve a sense of movement. The posture was systematically codified by the sculptor Polyclitus, who prescribed the structure of the human body as resting on one leg, pushed a little to the rear, with the other leg bent at the knee and applying less pressure. The chest, while tilted backwards, was slightly bent also, and the head leaned to the side in the opposite direction of the chest. This counterposing of the members of the body, or contrapposto, was seen as the ideal way of expressing movement. Since the Renaissance, as the fascination with movement and its representation increased, a debate commenced not only over the best way to represent movement and change, but also which was the most advanced of the arts in representing the dynamic rather than the static state of the world. For the Mannerist artists, the "serpent-like figure" of the S motif "that resembles the form

flame of fire"—in other words the contrapposto motif of the human figure generalized more schematically and abstractly—was thought to express movement better than any other form.[8]

During the nineteenth century Gotthold Ephraim Lessing, in his famous book *Laocoon*, gave a new impetus to the debate about the representation of movement in the arts in terms of a given medium's time and space constraints. Lessing borrowed the term *pregnant* from British philosopher Shaftesbury to explain the unique challenges to the visual arts in implying time, events, and process. Discussing the human figure in art, Lessing used the term *pregnant* to describe a position suspended between past and future, implying a prior position and extrapolating a future one.[9]

As has already been mentioned, Calatrava appears to push his structures to the optimal state between total success and failure, the

"critical point" between solid permanence and violent disappearance. But he also succeeds in uniting the engineer's critical point—making things stand in the most efficient manner—with the artist's concept of the "pregnant moment"—creating a cognitive experience from immobile objects. He achieves this feat through the visual experiments carried out in the repertory of moving figures drawn in the notebooks. Calatrava's notebooks reveal a designer who rejoices in the body in motion, like a dancer or an acrobat, and he strives to infuse that same joy into his structures, inspiring wonder while always remembering the quest to repair the disorder of the world.

Calatrava's notebooks reveal a designer who rejoices in the body in motion, like a dancer or an acrobat.

Drawings from
Calatrava's notebooks

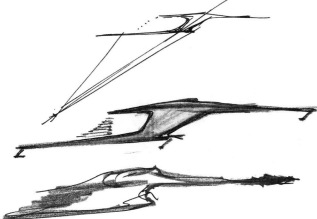

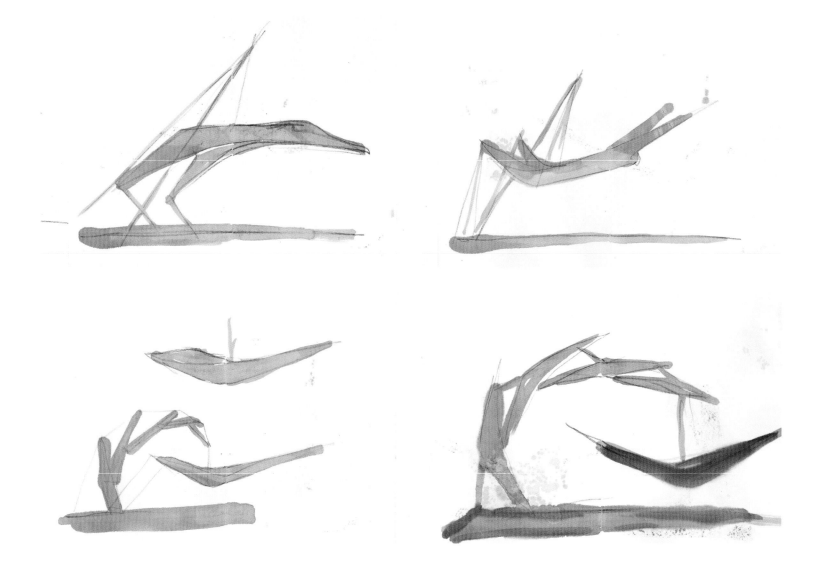

Drawings from
Calatrava's notebooks

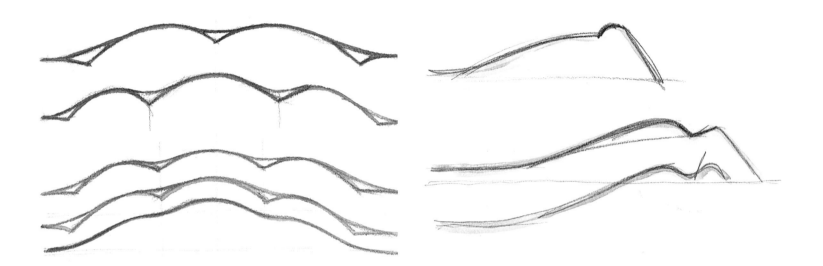

Drawings of roof forms
from Calatrava's
notebooks

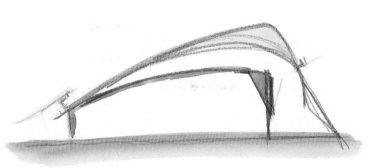

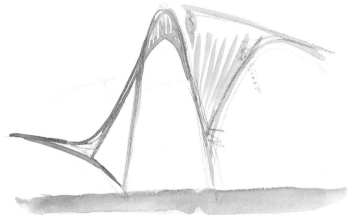

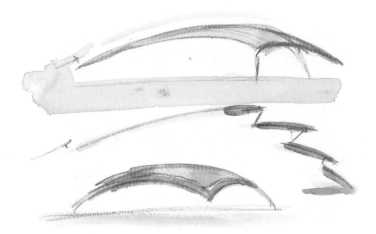

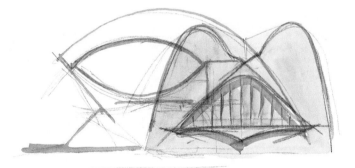

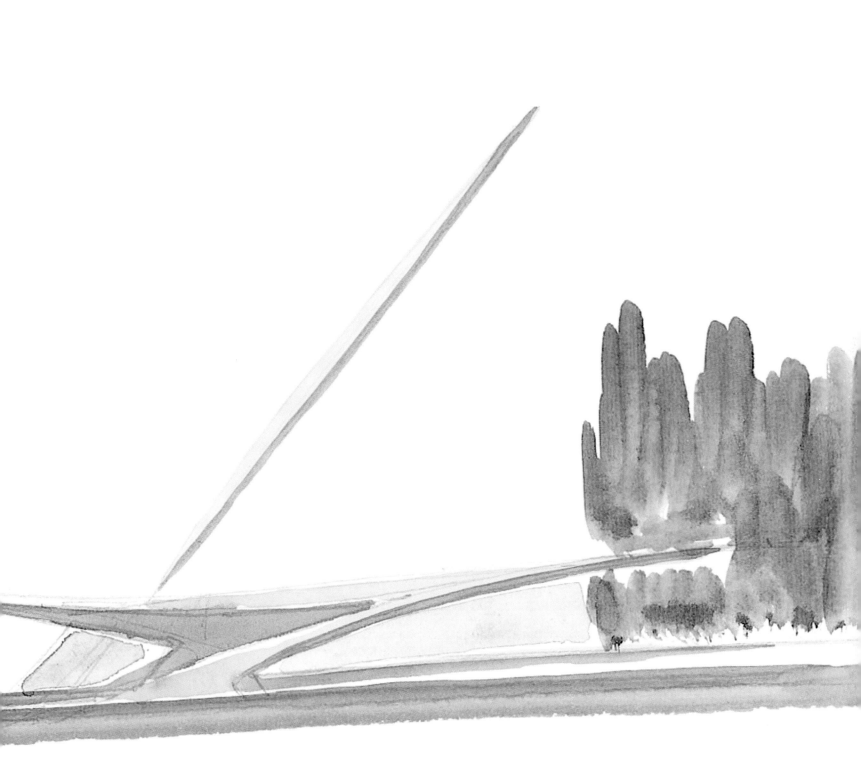

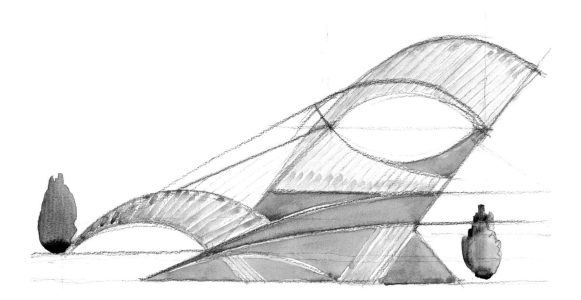

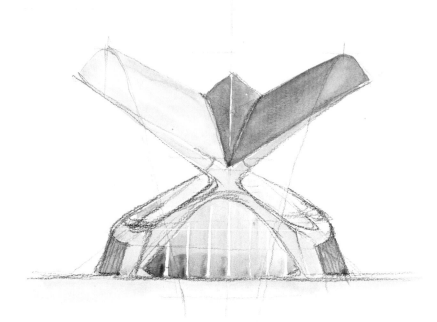

Previous pages, this
page, and opposite:
Structures in the land-
scape, by Calatrava

Structures in the land-
scape, by Calatrava

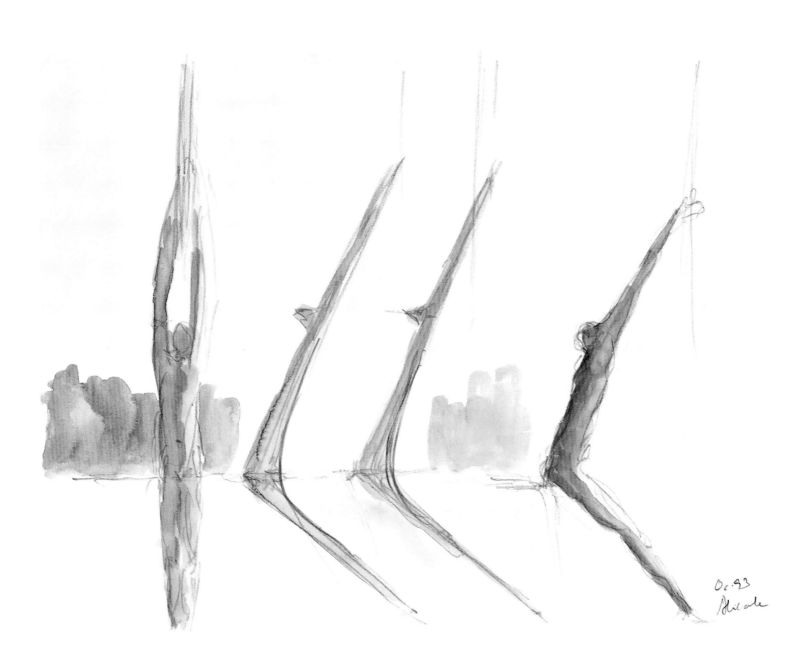

Chapter 4 | Morphogenetic Movements

Rarely has a designer succeeded in uniting analysis and analogy so happily to create such a rich variety of innovative projects as Calatrava has done. And rarely has such a variety of technologically and morphologically innovative projects emerged from their natural or cultural landscape as have most of the structures designed by Calatrava. The project for BCE Place, Toronto, Canada, for example, is equally indebted to the analytical studies on folding structures carried out by Calatrava in his dissertation and to extended analogies drawn from trees and medieval vaulting contained in the pages of the notebooks.

Originally, the competition to design BCE Place for the Brookfield Development Corporation required a small number of modest elements of high-quality urban design. The plan had developed in response to the "Percent for Public Art" program of the Public Arts Commission established by the Council of the City of Toronto in 1986. The program requested improvements to the former cultural and civic heart of Toronto, which was now intended for commercial development. In a move reminiscent of Le Corbusier's proposals for similar projects, Calatrava designed a major urban scheme that entirely redefines the character of the urban fabric, environmentally and socially. His proposal consisted of a huge, freestanding gallery penetrating the block from east to west and a striking roof over Heritage Square that offers protection from the weather but also integrates the minor residual spaces between existing buildings on the site. His scheme was accepted.

The continuous roof structure as it was finally built is 130 meters long, 14 meters wide, and 27 meters high. The arcade connects Heritage Square, the Canada Trust Tower lobby, the relocated classicist Clarkson Gordon Building, Garden Court, and Bay Street. Its arcade, with a canopy that emerges between the row existing of buildings to confront Mies van der Rohe's Toronto Dominion Center, acts as a pointer indicating the entrance to Toronto's subterranean pedestrian network, giving to a sense of identity. Escalators aligned along the main gallery's central axis allow access, and a circular fountain composed of steel tubes opening like a flower, also designed by Calatrava, marks the heart of the space. The colonnade is composed of supports that branch out to form the main linear passage. The geometry of the transparent vaults that rhythmically span the space derives not only from the studies on structures in Calatrava's dissertation but also from the vaulting of the Lonja de la Seda in Valencia and the fan vaulting of English cathedrals.

This page: View of site context. Opposite: Detail view of roof between buildings

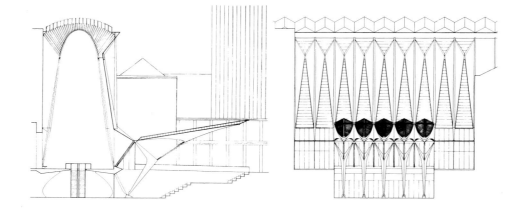

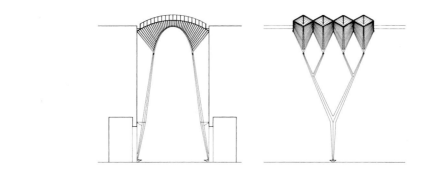

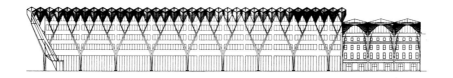

Sección longitudinal / *Longitudinal section*

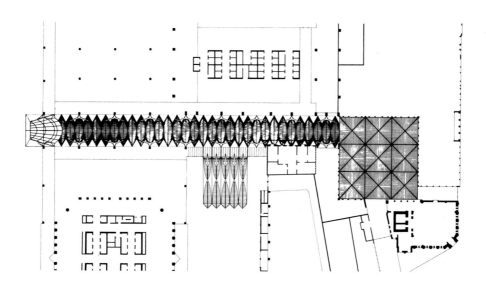

This page: Sections and
plan of the intervention.
Opposite: View through
gallery

While major opportunities for demanding urban complexes requiring significant engineering input similar to that for BCE Place in Toronto started to open up for Calatrava, the design of bridges—or the rethinking of their design—remained his key concern. The success of the seminal Bach de Roda bridge was followed by the scheme for the Caballeros Footbridge project, where the concept of a cable-stayed bridge with a single tilted pylon was executed with the steel-headed pylon cantilevered off a reinforced concrete support built at one bank of the river. The idea was elaborated further in the bridge for Pontevedra, Spain (1987). But it was in a bridge for the 1992 World's Fair in Seville that these innovations were fully developed.

The fair provided the authorities of Seville with an opportunity to improve the infrastructure of the city and its surrounding areas in the province of Andalusia. For Calatrava it was an opportunity to realize his ideas about the possibilities for infrastructure to function as a cultural object and for bridges to become works of art. Commissioned by La Junta de Andalucía as part of its World's Fair program, the Alamillo Bridge was executed within a general framework of improvements of road connections to neighboring towns, a ring road for Seville, and eight new bridges over the Guadalquivir River. The bridge spans 200 meters over the section of the river known as the Meandro San Jerónimo and is connected to a viaduct for automobiles, bicyclists, and pedestrians that crosses La Cartuja Island. Andalusian officials conceived the bridge to improve connections between Seville and its neighboring towns, but they also expected from the beginning that the bridge would be a landmark and the symbol of new development in the region.

The Alamillo site is unusual in that the same river is crossed twice. In response to this setting, Calatrava initially proposed two bridges with a pair of asymmetrical, 142-meter-high pylons to span the two sections of the river. The mirror image bridges, with their pylons tilted toward each other, approximately 1.5 kilometers apart and connected by the Cartuja Viaduct, would have suggested a huge triangle, its apex high in the sky.

The idea was not accepted. Further developing ideas conceived during the design of the Pontevedra Bridge, Calatrava proposed a new type of cable-stayed bridge with a single 142-meter-high pylon inclined at an angle of 58 degrees. The weight of the pylon is sufficient to counterbalance the deck, eliminating the need for backstays; instead, thirteen pairs of stay cables from the single pylon support the bridge. The core of the pylon tower contains a service stair to the top. The pylon was constructed by lifting segments of the steel shell into place with a large, high-capacity crane, then welding them together and filling them with reinforced concrete.

The bridge deck consists of a hexagonal, steel boxbeam spine, to which the stay cables are attached. The steel wings, supporting the deck at either side, are cantilevered off this spine, whose 3.75-meter-wide top side, elevated some 1.6 meters above road level, serves as an elevated footway and cycle route between the separated traffic lanes. Special attention was paid to the introduction of natural light, which flows through three continuous rows of circular light wells, one along the crown of the vault between the two roadways, and the other two at the sides, between the roadway and the promenades.

Completed in thirty-one months, the bridge was instantly recognized as a modern icon for a city with a remarkable history. Calatrava attributed part of the bridge's aura of monumentality to the fact that the pylon leans at the same angle as the slope of the pyramid of Cheops. The bridge's appearance of being suspended within the "pregnant moment" between permanence and collapse also contributes to its sublime profile.

Side view

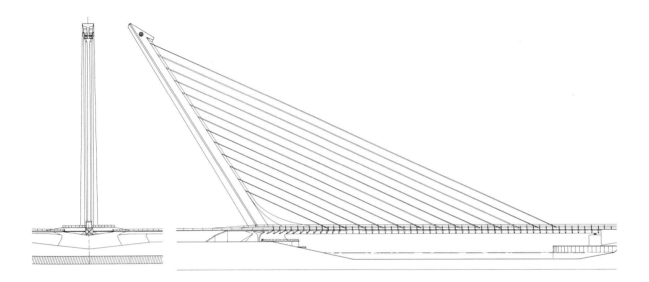

Elevation and view
from river bank

plstic 1   plstic 2   pnt d Schill

en ste capitul se splora la scala por jyel
Cambio de escala   el mismo persnaje a
                              dikts scals a realidz
[sketch of human figures in decreasing size]   i fgur de ella pra
                              etapa definitive.

definicin del proyet del pte d Schille

Preliminary sketches
by Calatrava

Designed in 1988, a year after the Alamillo, and completed in 1991, the Lusitania Bridge in Mérida, Spain, is a striking example of a modern infrastructure project successfully integrated into a demanding natural and historical landscape (the 2,000-year-old, 600-meter-long Roman bridge La Akazaba is still in operation). In contrast to the soaring pylon of the Alamillo Bridge, which overlooks rather dispersed surroundings, the Lusitania Bridge seen from a distance keeps a relatively level profile. Like the Cascine Bridge project in Florence, Italy—designed at the same time as the Alamillo and intended to occupy a site rich in history as well—the structure of the Lusitania Bridge is dominated by the gentle curve of its central steel arch spanning all 189

meters of the crossing. The intricacy of the structure is perceived only when one approaches the work more closely. Yet, like the Alamillo Bridge, its sweeping streamlined shape implies movement, albeit slower.

According to the project brief, the objective of the bridge's construction was to connect the old town of Mérida in west central Spain to the newly developed area of Poligono on the northern side of the Guadiana River and divert motor traffic from the old Roman bridge, which would become a footbridge.

The central load-bearing element of the bridge is its box girder—a torque tube 4.5 meters deep constructed from posttensioned, precast concrete elements. This element supports the

loads of the dual roadway along each of its sides. The loads of the bridge's approaches are delivered to reinforced concrete piers, which are spaced 45 meters apart. Within the center span, this box girder is suspended from the steel-tied arch by twenty-three steel rod pairs. Prestressed concrete wings, supporting the road decks, cantilever from the concrete box girder and are posttensioned to it. The upper surface of the box girder serves as a 5.5-meter-wide roadway for pedestrians and cyclists. Raised centrally above the dual carriageways, it passes through the concrete supports designed as portals for the bridge's arch. This elevated passageway offers the opportunity of unobstructed panoramic views of the landscape.

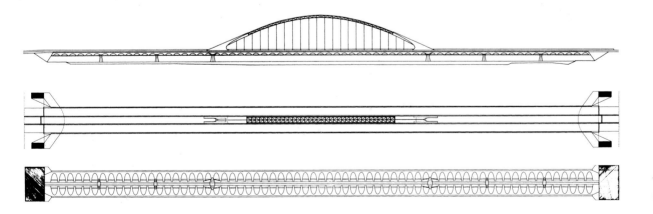

This page: Elevation, plan, and view up to bridge. Opposite: Drawing by Calatrava. Overleaf: Lusitania Bridge with the ancient Roman bridge La Akazaba in foreground

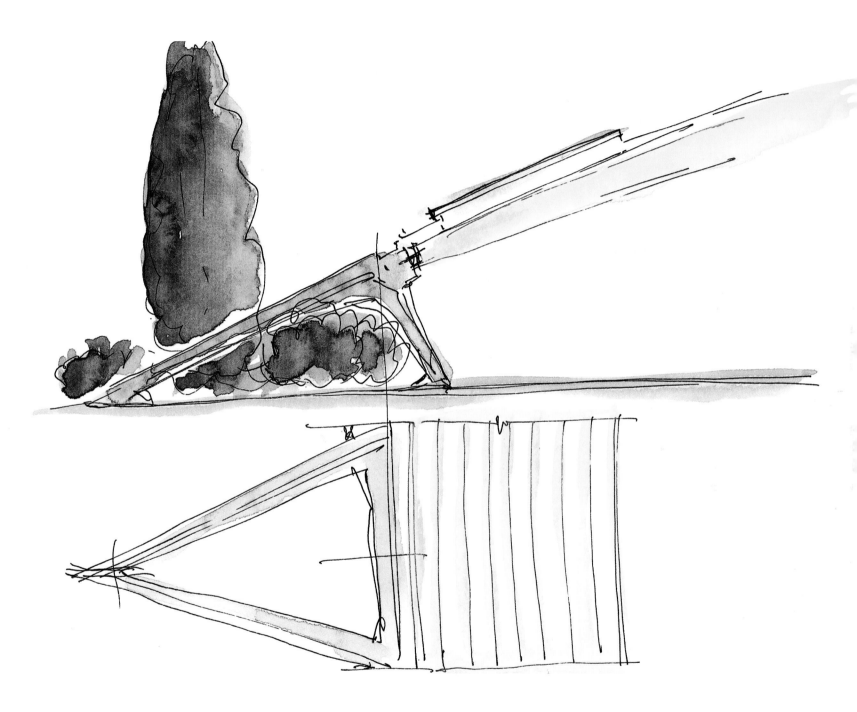

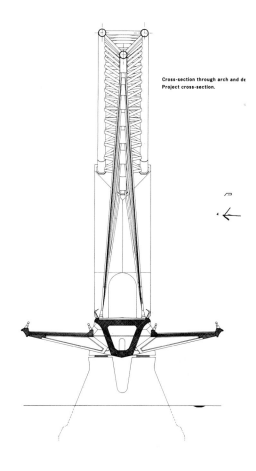

Cross-section through arch and de
Project cross-section.

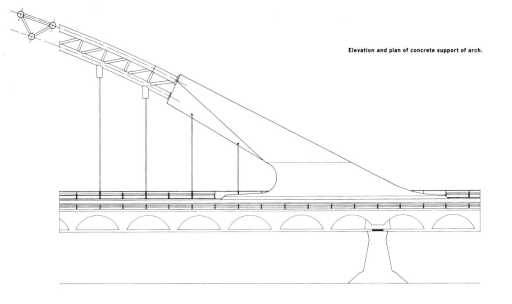

Elevation and plan of concrete support of arch.

This page: Drawing
of concrete supports
for arch (left); section
showing pedestrian and
vehicle paths (right).
Opposite: Bridge during
construction

| Collserola Telecommunications Tower Barcelona, Spain

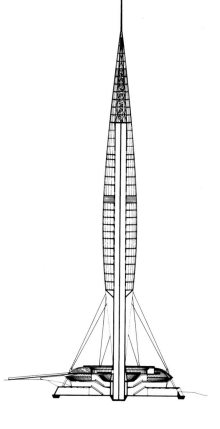

Another example of an infrastructure project that immerses itself into and enhances the landscape, despite its cutting-edge industrial construction, high-tech function, gigantic size, and rigorous geometric character, is the Collserola Telecommunications Tower in the Collserola hills of Barcelona, Spain. The project was the result of an invited limited competition and like the Alamillo Bridge it was linked with an event of international character, the 1992 Summer Olympic Games in Barcelona.

The goal of Barcelona's mayor was to reduce the number of miscellaneous communications towers and masts around the city by consolidating their functions into a single tower to be located on the Tibidabo, one of the Sierra Collserola hills that border the old city toward the north. Calatrava proposed a circular concrete shaft, 252 meters high and 7 meters in diameter, to carry the cantilevered steel service and equipment platforms with a maximum diameter of 22 meters. The structure was to be covered with a blue skin of synthetic material. The hovering, streamlined mast was stabilized by pairs of steel cable stays attached at a height of 91 meters and anchored to the circular base. All services and administrative facilities were placed within the base structure.

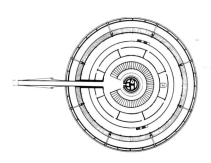

This page: Photomontage of tower on the hills (left); plan and section through shaft (right). Opposite: View of model

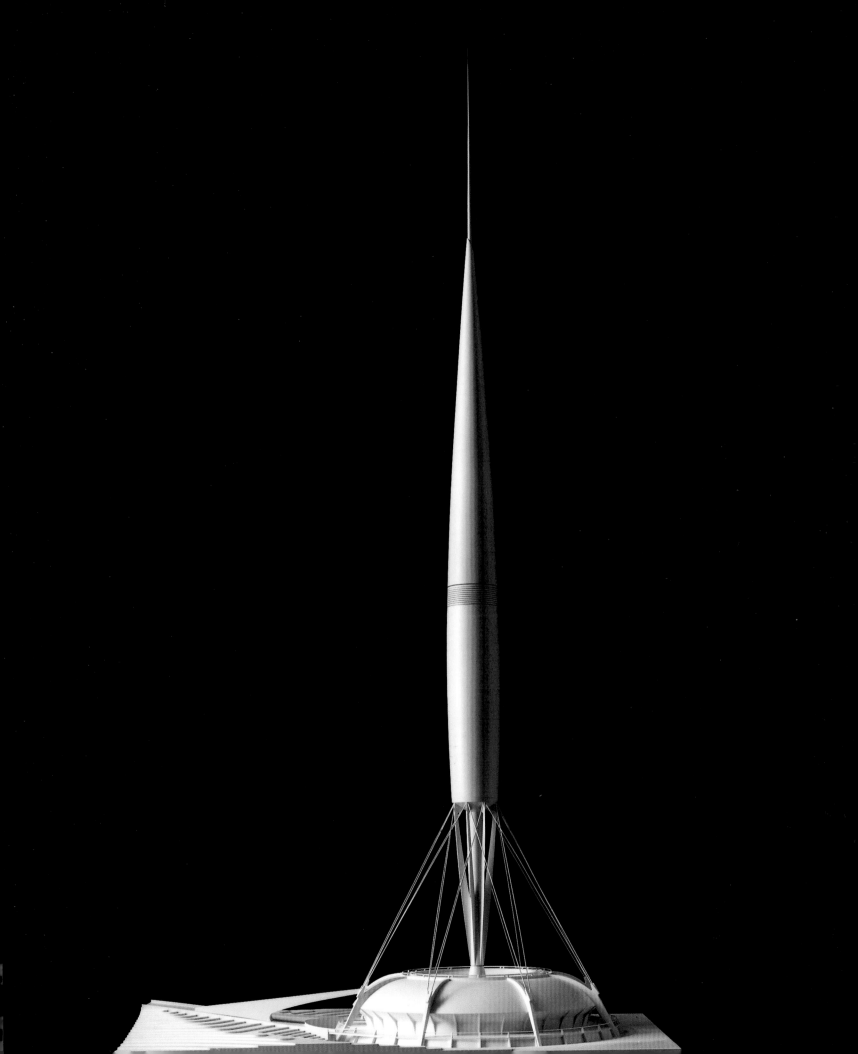

For the 1992 Summer Olympic Games in Spain, Calatrava proposed the Montjuic Telecommunications Tower. The tower was to be placed on the slopes of Montjuic Hill, in Barcelona overlooking the main group of sports facilities, immediately next to the Palau Sant Jordi Arena, designed by Arata Isozaki. Calatrava designed a 136-meter-high tower, leaning gently from a three-point foundation, with the tower's feet resting on a brick drum, a requirement of the competition. The base contains an articulated door, similar to the one used for the Ernsting Warehouse, to provide access to telecommunications services. A circular shell of white concrete supports the heel of the tower, which is covered by broken tiles, a regional traditional technique that was a quiet homage to Gaudí.

The tower creates a sense of scale, relating to the vast Olympic complex to the intimate pedestrian experience.

The tower structure offered a spatial reference point to a rather dispersed plan for the complex's facilities. Its leaning silhouette and circular segment containing the array of antennas with a needle suspended in the center is drawn by analogy from a human figure holding a rod—an obvious allusion to the Olympic torch. The coincidence of the tower's angle with the angle of the sun at solstice—as in the case of the Alamillo Bridge—is intended to give the tower and site greater cosmic significance. However, the tower's real impact is in the potential movement implied by the contrapposto profile and in its regenerative message.

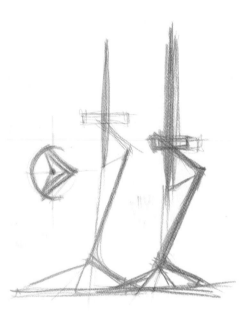

This page: Preliminary sketches by Calatrava. Opposite: Tower with surrounding Olympic complex

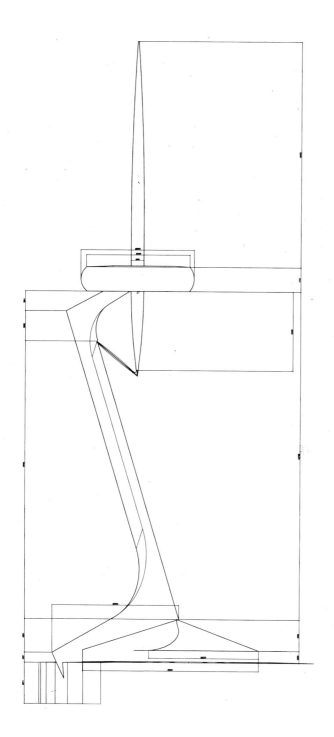

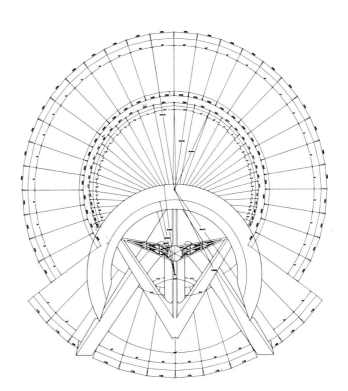

This page: Elevation
(left) and plan (right).
Opposite: Detail of base

Calatrava's treatment of movement has either been implicit in the structure of his projects—as in the Montjuic Tower—or confined to an embedded foldable structure of a door—as in the Ernsting Warehouse. For the open-air Bauschänzli Restaurant for the city of Zurich, Switzerland, Calatrava proposed a roof system whose pattern was a development of the tree

motif in BCE Place, which was not static but foldable. While the folding mechanism for the restaurant was drawn from the analytical investigations of the dissertation, the treelike figures emerged by analogy from a natural prototype, an analogy with happy allusions to the green of the high trees on the island site located in the River Limmat.

Calatrava's proposed foldable roof cover is composed of nine interlocking umbrella-like elements made out of glass and steel. Each element of the system is 12 meters high and functions as four articulated glazed leaves, which hinge upward along eight edges to define the outline of a star. When unfolded, the inclining planes create a continuous roof.

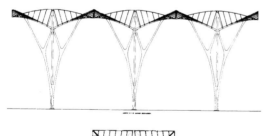

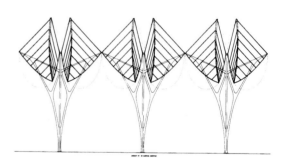

This page: Drawings showing the roof folding mechanism. Opposite: View of model

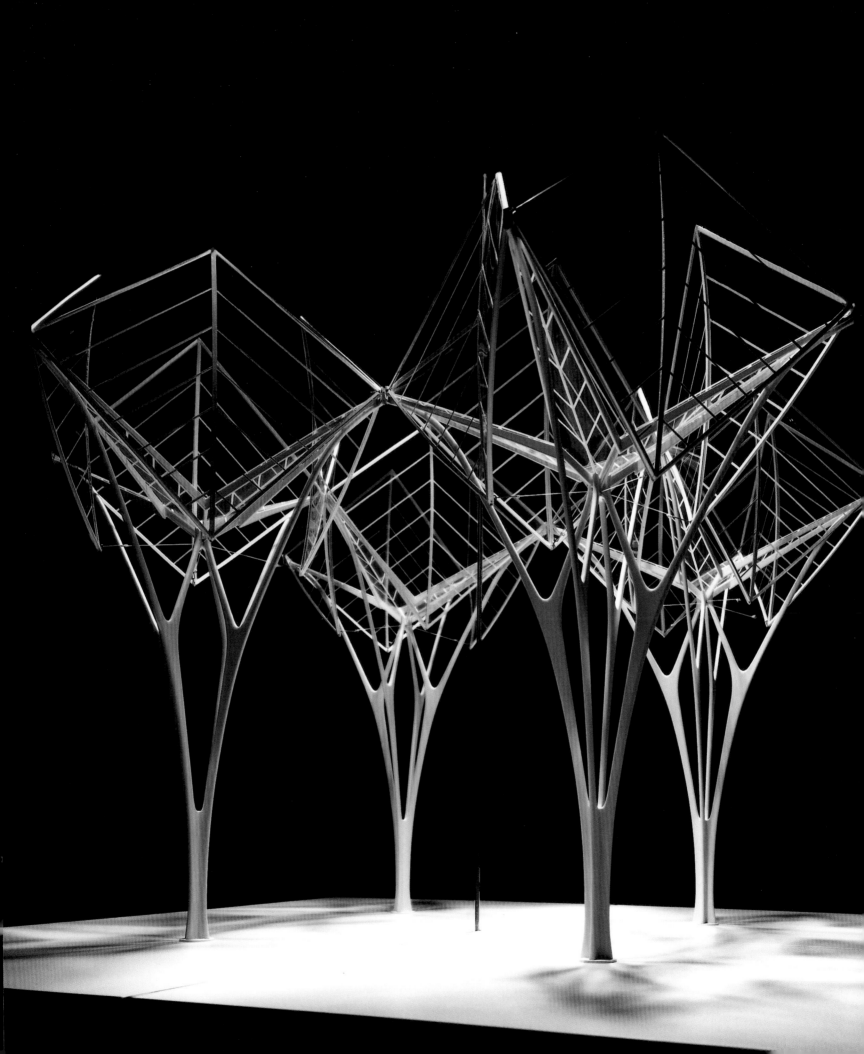

Calatrava's idea of folding structure was further developed for the roof of the Emergency Services Center, St. Gallen, Switzerland, a twenty-four-hour facility from which the canton's traffic system is coordinated. Every effort was made to respect the historical identity of this significant UNESCO-designated World Heritage site. The mass of the building was placed underground. The system of a movable roof based on rib-like slats and a mechanical hoist—used here for the first time—did not conflict with the surrounding structures despite its strong technological character. Reinforced glass elements 7 centimeters thick and weighing up to two tons were used for the roof, supporting themselves along the curved ridge of the structure's ribs. Because this glazed roof covers the central space containing the electronic control systems, light and temperature control are essential. The project also included the Pfalzkeller Gallery, a multipurpose facility for cultural and social events consisting of three rooms: an underground, semicircular space for concerts, lectures, conferences, and exhibitions, adjacent to the wine cellars of a neighboring monastery; an art gallery; and a court cellar accessible through a subterranean passage and from the side of the monastery. The themes of Calatrava's poetics of movement, relating as they so often do to objects belonging to the aerial or aquatic worlds, appear to adapt excellently to this chthonic environment, especially as they employed in such close proximity to the famous and historically rich monastery where the manuscript of Vitruvius that would change the path of modern Western architecture was discovered during the early Renaissance.

Interior of the central space

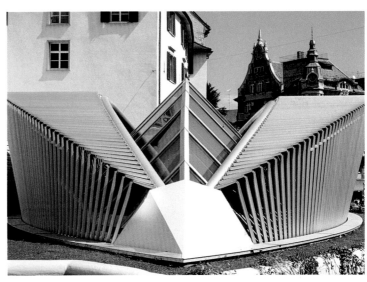

This page: Folding roof
in operation. Opposite:
View of project with sur-
rounding urban context

Top left and opposite:
Views of entrance
through subterranean
passage when open
and closed. Bottom left:
Interior

Calatrava further developed the folding roof structure on a much larger scale, and requiring greater technological performance, in the Zurich University Law Faculty building in Switzerland. The project was conceived in 1989 and finished in 2004. For decades the growing requirements of Zurich University had been met through a program of expansion in Irchel Park, a beloved green area on the city's outskirts. More recently, the Building Surveyor's Office of the Canton of Zurich (the client for this project) and the university's planning department have adopted a revised policy to optimize existing facilities within the historic university quarter.

The project brief stated that the facilities for the Faculty and its library, with its distinguished and rare book collection (the second largest in the country), and currently dispersed throughout eight different buildings, were to be centralized and greatly expanded. The original, L-shaped structure was designed by Hermann Fiertz in 1908 as a high school and laboratory. Two wings, which do not reach the height of the original structure, were added in 1930 to create a central courtyard.

In 1989, Calatrava was commissioned to prepare a study that would include the addition of two stories to the 1930 wings, bringing them to the height of the original L-shaped building, to house administrative offices and classrooms. The university's brief envisioned the full use of the cluttered courtyard. Rather than obliterate the courtyard under several floor slabs, Calatrava developed a strategy of "densification," proposing a supplemental structure within the original volume to redefine the courtyard as an atrium.

Calatrava produced several proposals and in the final design reached a solution composed of individual, optimally equipped work spaces for the students, with direct access to the library levels and seminar spaces. A seven-level series of oval galleries containing the reading areas are hung within the atrium, staggered so that the space circumscribed within each level increases as they rise. In this configuration natural light can penetrate deeper into the heart of the structure and its reading areas, an important feature of the concept. To support the cascade

of galleries, eight attachment points have been created within or against the walls of the existing facade. The basic structure of each gallery is formed by a steel torsion tube, from which T-shaped, tapering steel beams cantilever in a regular rhythm. Each gallery is braced by ballustrades, which have been designed as load-bearing trusses. By channeling the forces away from the center of the atrium, this design also leaves the basement areas free of obstruction.

The roof is a glazed skylight with steel mullions supporting the glazed panels. Its geometry is based on the surface of revolution of an elliptical arc. Flexible and efficient shading was imperative, and to respond optimally to these severe demands, two expanses of canvas, one on each side of the roof's center line, are tensioned by valley weights and fixed to the curve of the main roof support as well as to an arched steel tube that rotates around the same axis as the skylight form. A cable mechanism pulls the two tubes independently up toward the apex of the roof to open the shade and allow more light to filter into the building.

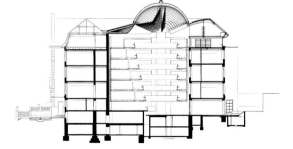
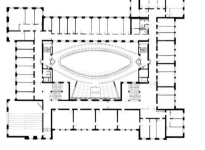

This page: Section and plan. Opposite: View of folding roof structure

1989 | **CH-91 Pavilion** Lucerne, Switzerland

Calatrava's moving roof theme is explored further in the project for the CH-91 Pavilion on Lake Lucerne, Switzerland. The client was the Swiss Cement Association, which had already commissioned Calatrava to design the Swiss-bau Pavilion (to be discussed in the next chapter). Calatrava conceived a sculpture for this occasion that served as a laboratory exploring the geometry of the elements and mechanisms of movement that led to this project's architectural form. The design was also intended as a further experiment in the use of concrete. Calatrava suggested a floating island that could be guided to any site on the shores of Lake Lucerne. An auditorium, exhibition space, and other facilities were to be included to enliven the small lakeside communities in the area, which were poorly equipped for large-scale public events.

The roof of the pavilion consisted of twenty-four mobile, precast concrete petal-shaped elements arranged in a radial pattern, representing the twenty-four cantons of Switzerland. The opening flower theme was further advanced in roofs for later projects including the Reichstag, in Berlin, and the Kuwait Pavilion in Seville.

Views of the mechanically operating roof closed and open

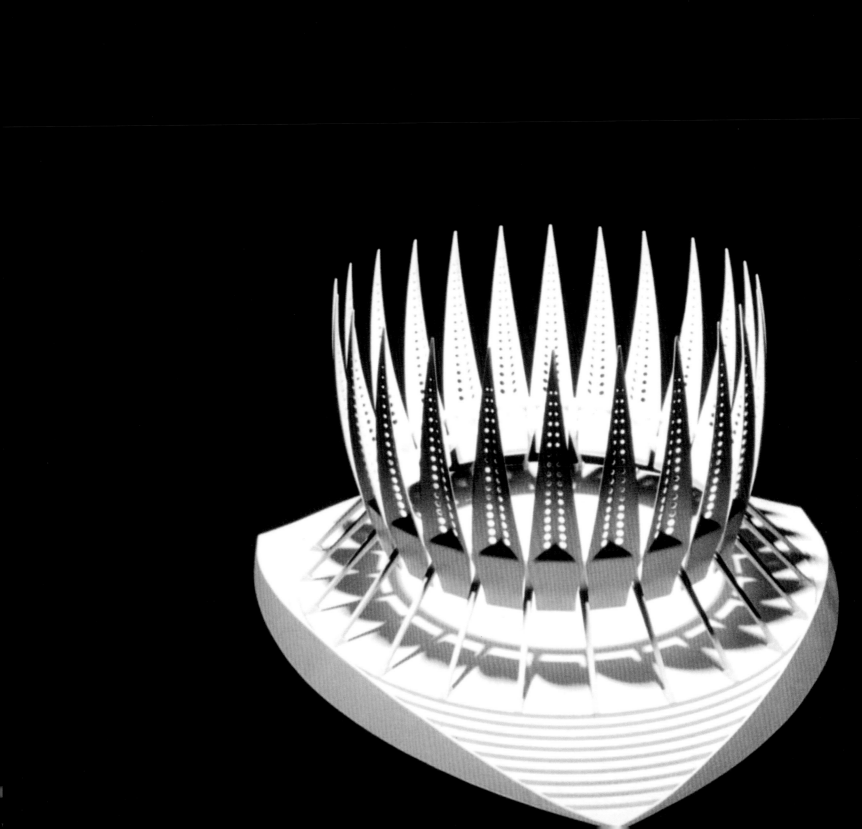

Calatrava received the commission for the Lyons Airport Station, Satolas, France, through an invitational competition organized by the Rhône-Alpes Region and Lyons Chamber of Commerce and Industry (CCIL) as part of a drive to boost trade through improved transportation. The Lyons Airport Station was the terminus of a new rail connection between Lyons and the Saint-Exupéry Airport in Satolas. The competition brief called for a building that would provide smooth passenger flow while creating an exciting and symbolic "gateway to the region." Designed in 1989, the station was constructed by 1994. Rather than orienting travelers by way of signs giving directions within neutral "universal space containers," as often happens in contemporary air and ground transportation terminals, Calatrava opted for a highly differentiated arrangement of specialized pockets marking the identity and position of spaces through the configuration of the enclosure. This proved to be not only effective in guiding crowds of travelers to their

destination but also revived civic and ritualistic aspects of public transportation celebrated in the 1900s—as in the famous Gare de Lyons of Paris—and forgotten in the recent past.

At the entrance on the upper deck, a concrete, V-shaped abutment joins the ends of four steel arches as they lunge forward to greet the visitor. The center pair follows the line of the roof to form a spine composed of baffled vertebrae. The adjacent pair of curved beams spans 120 meters over a towering glazed station hall and eastern service core containing ticket offices, retail shops, and other amenities. This multilevel service block also houses the stationmaster's office, the airport police, and offices and technical areas for the French Rail System and the CCIL. The service concourse is connected to the airport by a raised, 180-meter steel gallery, which in turn connects to a covered extension for pedestrian access to the parking garage, underground service area, and elevators. Bus and taxi terminals are located to the west. The vertebrae rise over the north and

south facades, whose bulging mullions support the cantilevered span. Concrete bridges, stairs, escalators, and glass elevators provide access to the platforms. Four tracks serve the station—two on each side of the central walkway—and provision has been made for two further tracks outside the platform hall to serve "Satorail," the future regional connection to Lyons. The structure has been cast in situ, including the recesses for light fittings. The concrete has a natural color through the use of a local white sand mix. The roof above the platforms is either glazed or filled with prefabricated concrete slabs.

Like the Zurich station, but also like prior projects by Eero Saarinen mimicking the skeletal structure of birds, Calatrava's design for Satolas represents streamlined figures virtually and latently in motion. Movement is present in the profile and arrangement of the elements of the structure rather than through mechanical objects, transforming travel from a dreary necessity into a memorable celebration of movement.

Opposite: Detail of
roof above platforms.
Overleaf: Exterior view

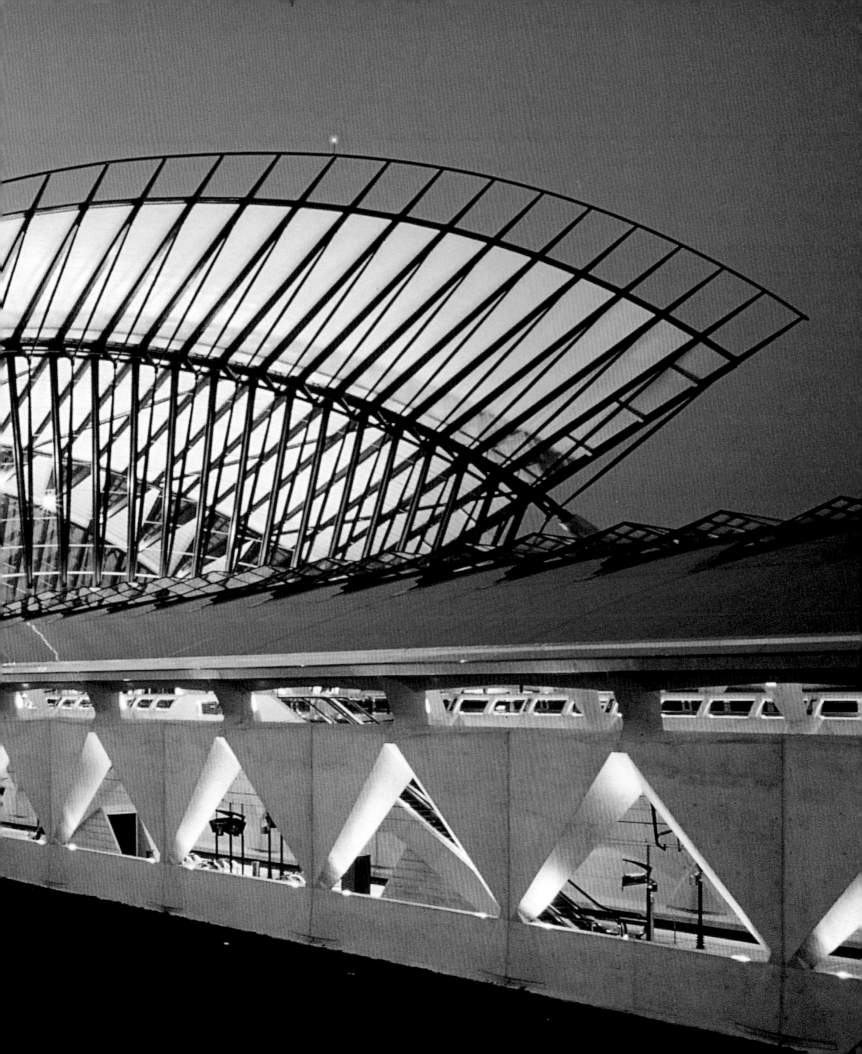

This page: Detail of
structure and section.
Opposite: Concrete
abutment

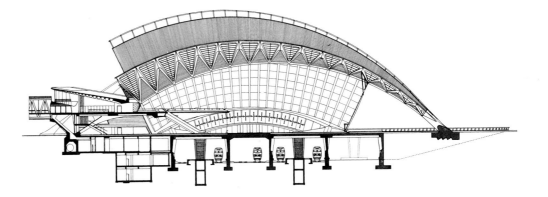

View toward west entrance

View toward east entrance
with cantileverd galleries

View of walkway above
railway tracks

View of station platforms

In contrast to the Satolas Station—in an open field where identity of place requires a robust spatial configuration—the Puerto Bridge, Ondarroa, Spain, is inserted into an existing community surrounded by a delicate landscape. The structure is simple and elegant but rewarding. It delicately balances a single arch spanning 71 meters over the port of Ondarroa, at the mouth of the Artibay River. The deck defines yet integrates two 4.5-meter-wide pedestrian walkways with a 7-meter-wide vehicular crossing. The 15-meter-deep asymmetric steel arch carries both the box-girder vehicular deck and the curved, canti-levered pedestrian deck. While the arch takes vertical loads from stay cables, it is braced against buckling by inclined tension arms loaded by the sheer weight of the seaside pedestrian walkway. Although the three passageways have a consistent width, the seaside walkway bows outward to trace a semicircle; as the deck raises in height, the cantilever also increases as it nears the midpoint of the bridge. This banked surface creates an important space in relation to the rest of the bridge floor. Structurally, the extension counterbalances the opposite side of the bridge precisely where more support is needed—at the midpoint.

The structure, with its recognizable geometry, makes a significant contribution to the landscape's own soft, fractal geometry. Seen from some distance above, the circular elements of the bridge echo the curves of the harbor and town. Seen from below, they reflect the gentle curves of the surrounding hills. As with Ronchamp, one becomes more aware of the character and the uniqueness of the landscape through the presence of the sculpture-structure of the bridge. At the same time, the bridge's identifiable shape provides a focal point that enhances the place's sense of community.

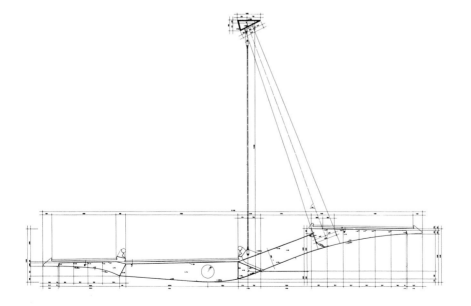

This page: Construction drawing, section. Opposite: View from below showing connection to the ground. Overleaf: Bridge in landscape

Commissioned by the town of Ripoll, north of Barcelona, Spain, in the Pyrenees, La Devesa Footbridge was designed in 1989 and constructed between August 1990 and July 1991. The bridge crosses a 44-meter span and accommodates a 5-meter grade change to connect the area of La Devesa with the town's railway station. The solution uses a structural idea already developed in the Gentil Bridge project for Paris: steel tension arms lying within the plane of the arch absorb the walkway loads. These arms are set at an angle of 65 degrees, so that their tensioning includes both horizontal and vertical components. While the vertical component stems from the dead and live loads, the horizontal component is developed by a cross-truss, which lies directly beneath the walkway and prevents it from distorting laterally. Because the weight of the timber-surfaced deck is not centered beneath the arch, it will tend to rotate, together with the tension arms, into a position of equilibrium below the arch. This rotation is prevented by the torque of the tubular steel spine of the bridge, which collects torsion at each strut and delivers it to the springing points: the pylon and the retaining wall. The tension arms brace the plane of the arch, preventing it from buckling. As gravity loads tend to deflect walkway and tension arms, the arch is displaced to a more vertical position, slightly stiffening it and protecting it against buckling. The bridge functions as an elegant discourse on the act of balancing, a concise but sophisticated essay on the art of negotiating countering action through the hardware of infrastructure to offer a solution that contrasts but is respectful of the rather desolate character of the site.

This page: Construction drawing, section. Opposite: Bridge at dusk

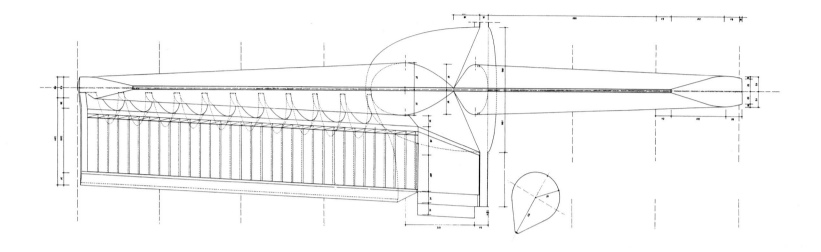

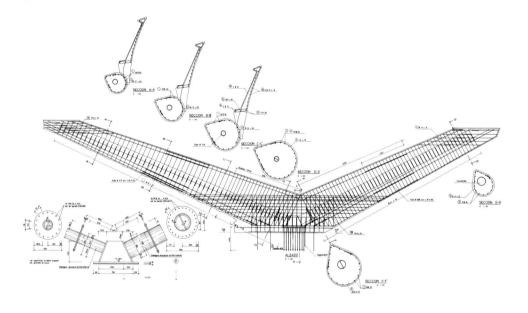

This page: Plan of pylon and staircase (above); engineer's drawing of reinforced concrete pylon (below). Opposite: General view with railway station in background

A similar message from La Devesa Footbridge appears in the Volantin Footbridge, Bilbao, Spain. The sophisticated strangeness of its parabolic configuration challenges the ordinariness and conventionality of its urban setting. An inclined, 14.6-meter-deep arch consisting of a pipe of 45.7 centimeters in diameter with a 50-millimeter thickness opposes the 75-meter boardwalk curve it supports. The sweeping parabolic form of the arch rests precariously on the extended armatures of the 2-meter-wide access ramp's triangular supports. Floating 8.5 meters over Bilbao's Nervión River with a width between 6.5 and 7.5 meters, the bridge's flooring consists of glass plates. Double-T shaped and 10 millimeters thick, a 70-centimeter-wide galvanized steel grid composed of forty-one steel ribs with variable sections runs along the outside of the glass flooring and supports the stainless steel profiles. As with the Alamillo Bridge, lighting plays an important role. The light sources are located between the steel ribs, illuminating the floor from underneath; additional lighting is placed in the handrails, stairs, and ramps. At night the illuminated bridge becomes a light sculpture—a beacon to enhance the surrounding community.

This page: Bridge at night lighted from underneath. Opposite: General view of bridge. Overleaf: View from riverside

In 1990, ten years after designing the Lyons Airport Station, Calatrava was asked to design a new airport for Bilbao, Spain, the existing facility having reached its limits. Located to the north of Bilbao on the coast of the Bay of Biscay, the initial facility accommodated only domestic flights and could not, therefore, function as a transportation hub for the growing Basque region. The Spanish airport authorities asked Calatrava to design a new terminal with four embarkation gates that would comply with international air-transport standards. A second proposal for passenger facilities, this time with a total of eight gates, was requested in 1994, to accommodate the increasing number of flights to this quickly developing area. The airport is connected by a 100-meter subterranean passageway to a four-story, partially recessed parking garage, which can accommodate 1,500 vehicles. A rail connection is planned from the new airport across the airfield to the original terminal. The project permits future expansion. The airport handles 2 million passengers per year, and that number will ultimately rise to 10 million. The way the project fits into the landscape and the rich variety of spaces that constitute the overall complex, show how Calatrava's poetics of movement in structures and his ideas about the poetry of travel have matured over the past two decades.

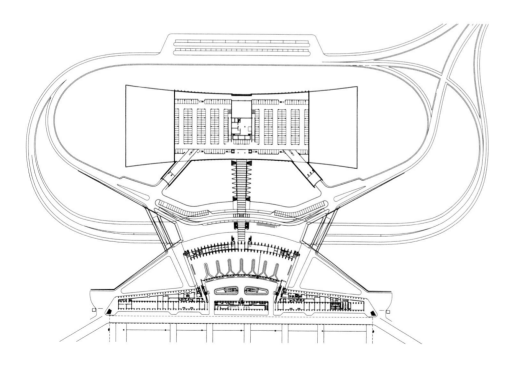

This page: Plan of ground floor. Opposite: Detail view of roof. Overleaf: Terminal building from airfield

Access from car park

Interior view of departures hall

The Tenerife Concert Hall, in the Spanish Canary Islands, was intended to provide a much needed facility for cultural events as well as an image for the site's evolving identity as a gateway to a new park in the western part of the city. The project, commissioned in 1991 and completed in 2003, grew as a result of a close collaboration between Calatrava and the local government of Tenerife.

The complex consists of an auditorium that seats 1,800 and a chamber music hall with seating for 400. The entrance for the artists is provided through wide arches, spanning 50 meters on each side of the structure. The entrance for the public is located on the raised plaza to the northeast, beneath the curved and sculpted concrete shell of the roof. Administration spaces, service areas, and the central auditorium are air-conditioned, while the public foyers and circulation areas feature ventilation, with air induced to flow through the glazed areas beneath and between the building's concrete shells to take full advantage of the island's pleasant climate.

Most of the richly differentiated volumes of this intricate compact composition were derived from relatively simple geometrical shapes or operations. For example, the shape of the roof is defined by two intersecting cone segments. The shape of the 50-meter-high symmetrical inner shell of the concert hall was generated by rotating a curve to describe an ellipse: a wedge of approximately 15 degrees was removed from the center of this body so that its two segments (60 centimeters thick for acoustical purposes) form a pronounced ridge that supports the sweep of the roof. The crystalline form of the interior wood paneling resulted from fine-tuning acoustical needs. The auditorium features a concertina screen of vertical aluminium slats, which upon opening rise and extend into the auditorium to act as a sound reflector above the orchestra pit and replace the function of stage curtains.

The use of concrete to construct the building's large-scale spaces allows its profile to be perceived from a greater distance, particularly the roof rising off the base like a crashing wave soaring 58 meters over the main auditorium before curving downward and narrowing to a point. This is perhaps the most extreme analogy implying movement ever generated by Calatrava. However, for the smaller-scale, more intimate areas of the building, basalt and volcanic stone are used to cover surfaces and offer a more local feeling.

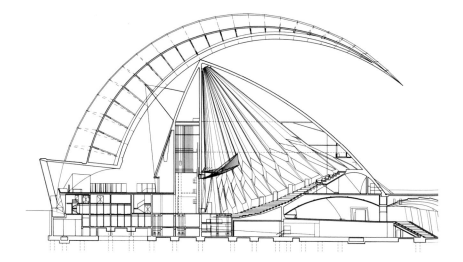

This page: Section through auditorium.
Opposite: Overall view

This page: View at dusk.
Opposite: The building
against the sea

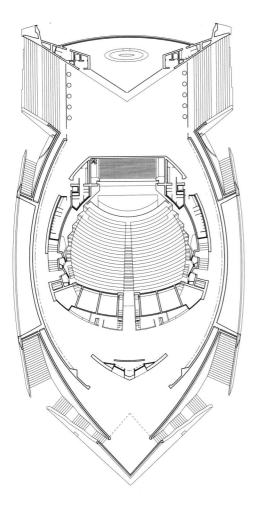

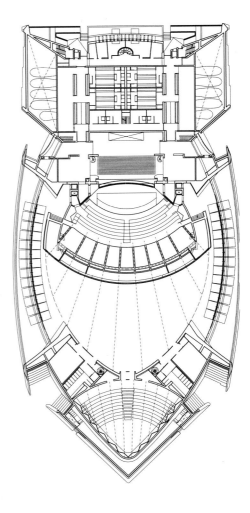

This page: Plan of first floor showing main entrance hall and auditorium (left); plan of ground floor showing artists' entrance and chamber music hall (right). Opposite: Interior of concert hall

Four views of raised plaza
beneath concrete shell

As with most Expo structures, one expects from the scheme of a pavilion to express the identity, regional, cultural, and historical, of the commissioning nation or institution. When Calatrava was commissioned in 1991 to design the Kuwait Pavilion for the 1992 World's Fair in Seville, he decided to cover the entire structure with a folding roof and to shape its moving components by analogy to the branches of a palm tree. The system of the moving roof advanced ideas worked out more theoretically for the unbuilt CH-91 Pavilion project.

A raised, 525-square-meter piazza terminating in two curvilinear walls features a surface that was a gentle barrel shape and is glazed with laminated structural glass panels superimposed with a thin layer of translucent marble.

Terraces of steps along each side of the structure conform to the curve of the glazed surface. Narrow, curving stairs follow the exterior shape of each endwall down to an enclosed exhibition space accessed through airfoil-sectioned revolving doors. The laminated surface of glass and marble is supported by arched trusses in the form of open, triangulated timber latticework. The trusses partially reuse the solution applied in the auditorium at the Wohlen High School. They spring at 2.4-meter intervals from the hollow, reinforced concrete beams that run the length of this formal exhibition space. The main exhibition floor, finished in a checkered marble pattern, is recessed within a white marble perimeter. At night floodlighting filters up through the piazza floor to provide soft illumination. By day

the exhibition area is indirectly lit by a calm sheen of light falling through the semitransparent, laminated ceiling, while triangular slotted patterns in the lower part of the terraced steps illuminate the peripheral areas. At the top of the terraced steps, two rows of equidistant, concrete supports (eight along one side, nine along the other) face each other across the glazed floor to support the building's main feature—the roof. Here seventeen scimitar-shaped ribs, each 25 meters in length, form the main articulated structure. Each rib is computer-controlled by a separate electric drive to open in fifteen preprogrammable positions up to the vertical and, when closed, to interlace with the others to form a cover, which repeats the slatted structure of the trusses spanning the space below.

View of pavilion

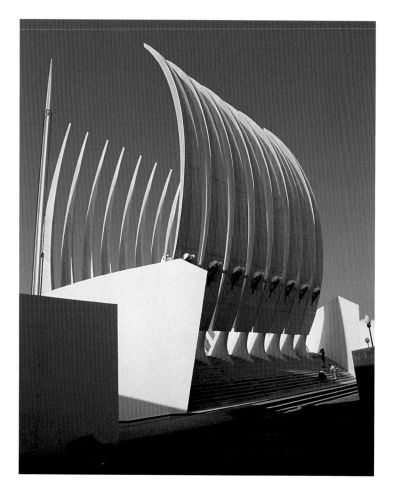

This page: Closed roof
seen from entrance.
Opposite: Views of
roof open and in half-
closed position

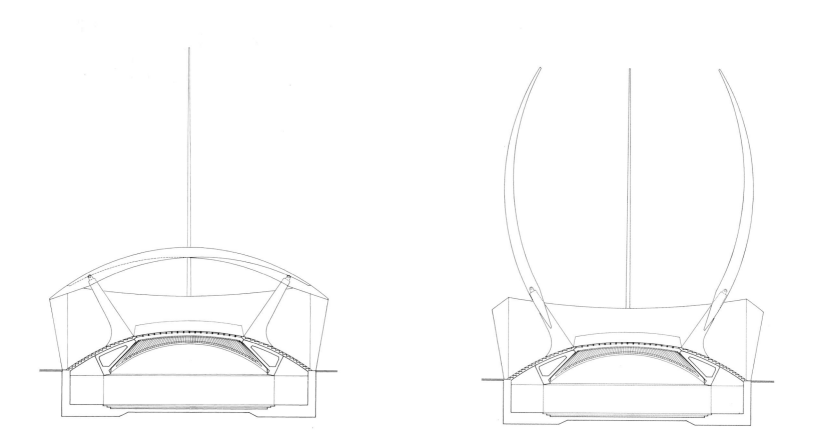

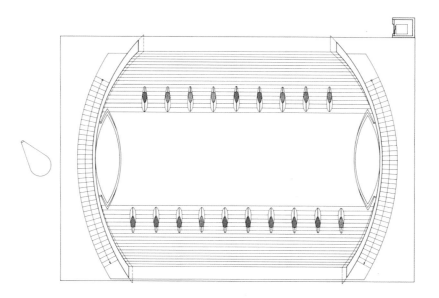

This page: Sections with roof closed and open (above); plan (below). Opposite: Preliminary sketches by Calatrava

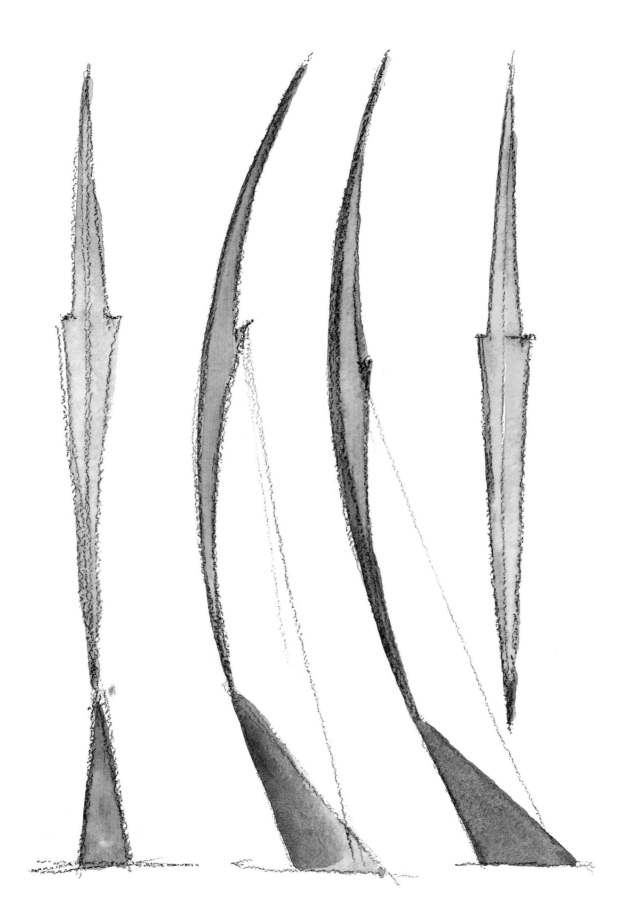

In 1991 Calatrava won a competition for a telecommunications tower to be built on a 35-hectare site located in the dry bed of the Turia River, midway between the old city of Valencia and the coastal district of Nazaret, in Spain. Calatrava subsequently received the commission to develop the whole complex, which was to be called the City of Arts and Sciences and would include a planetarium and a science museum. After a change of government in 1996, the planned telecommunications tower was replaced by an opera house. The planetarium in the City of Arts and Sciences in Valencia sits like a floating globe under a transparent concrete shell 110 meters long and 55.5 meters wide. The main building contrasts fixed and mobile metal structures: The concrete "lid" of the eye-shaped structure incorporates a system of slats mounted on each side of pivoting central stems. As the mobile parts of the structure open out, they reveal the interior of the sphere, giving it an appearance of lightness. Shallow reflecting pools surrounding the complex enhance the structure's sense of floating and wash over the library, cinema, auditorium, and restaurant facilities beneath.

The compound's science museum is 104 meters wide and 241 meters long, and it resembles the grand exhibition pavilions of the past created from the modular development of transverse sections that repeat along the length of the site. Five concrete trees, organized in a row, branch out to support the connection between roof and facade on a scale that permits the integration of service cores and elevators. The triangular structures that brace the ends of the building also mark the entrances. The white concrete supporting framework of the south facade is filled with glass; the north facade is a continuous glass-and-steel curtain along the building's full length.

The opera house provides Valencia with a major auditorium seating 1,300. In addition to opera productions the facility could be used for concerts, theater, and other performances. An additional open-air auditorium sheltered by a roof can seat up to 2,000 people and offers spectacular views of the complex. A fifth structure, known as L'Umbracle, functions as a promenade and parking garage and is built within an open arcade conceived as an updated winter garden of our time. A raised, axial walkway, offering views to the sea, serves as an ordering element, with gardens and reflecting pools on either side.

Detail view of planetarium

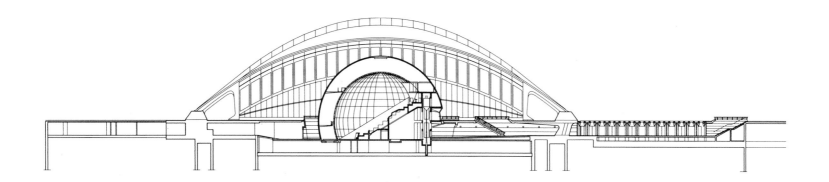

This page: View of concrete and glass canopy in operation. Opposite: View of planetarium with folding canopy (above); section (below). Overleaf: View of science museum

Interior view with
concrete "tree" structure

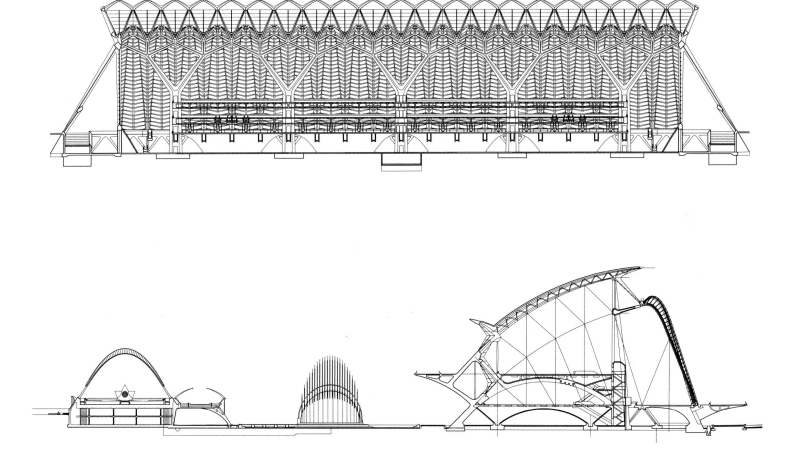

Longitudinal section
and cross section
with winter garden
and parking garage

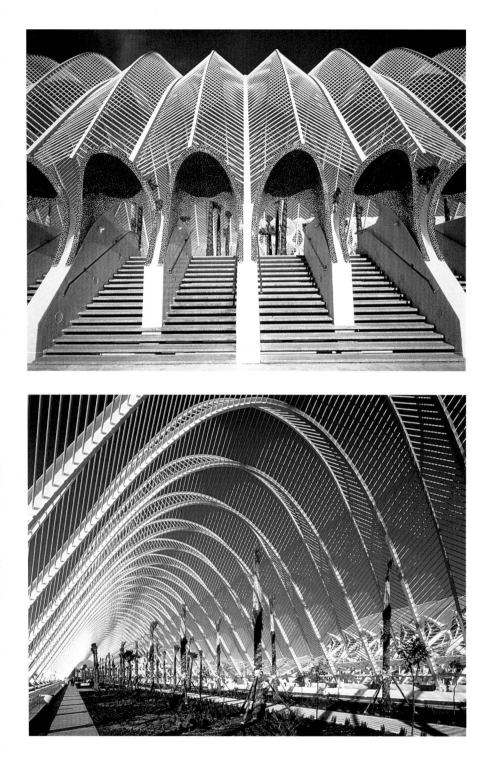

This page: Two views
of winter garden.
Opposite: Interior view
of science museum

The interesting aspect of the Alameda Bridge, in Valencia, Spain, is that it is combined with a subway station placed beneath the bed of the Turia River to create a single public infrastructure complex. Valencia has long been identified with the Turia, which throughout history has provided a natural defense for the city. But due to its frequent catastrophic flooding, and despite the impressive walls of the Masonic guild, the river's path was finally diverted in 1957, and the resulting tract of land was transformed into a linear park that runs through the city. The commission for the bridge and subway station was won by Calatrava through a competition in 1991.

The bridge spans 130 meters across the river with a structure that uses an inclined arch at an angle of 70 degrees. The deck includes two pedestrian walkways cantilevered on both sides of the vehicle deck.

The Alameda station, running on the same longitudinal axis of the river, was intended to become an important subway node for two lines meeting under the Turia riverbed. Calatrava originally proposed an open station with access at the northern and southern ends of a new bridge connecting the university campus with the old town. In a later proposal the entire station was covered to create an open space above ground.

The original proposal for the bridge was further modified to become a canted-arch scheme similar to the Gentil Bridge project for Paris. The presence of the subway is now suggested by the translucent glass–paved surface and by a series of protruding, angled skylights. Ramps and stairs on either side of the embankment lead to the subway. The platforms can be reached through elevators contained in the buttresses of the bridge or through escalators and stairs that are accessed through mechanical folding doors, which close flush with the paving to seal the station. At night light filters up from the subway level through the glass inlay to illuminate the bridge.

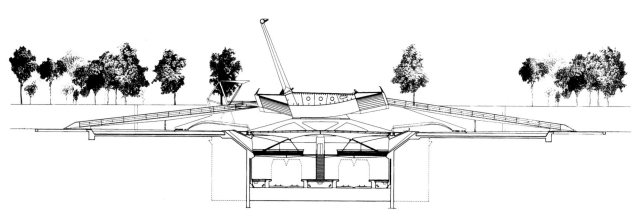

This page: Cross section. Opposite: View of subway station. Overleaf: Bridge at night

The project for the Cathedral of St. John the Divine in New York City, conceived for a competition won by Calatrava, reveals a great debt to medieval architecture. Construction of the Episcopal cathedral, located near Columbia University on Manhattan's Upper West Side, was begun in 1892. Originally a Romanesque design by the Boston firm of Heins & La Farge, the structure was later converted to a neo-Gothic style. Planned to become the largest cathedral in the world, it was never completed: the west towers, the crypt and piers of the north transept, the spire, and the south transept remain unfinished.

Since the construction of the cathedral's nave in 1939, there have been various attempts to complete the project in the spirit of address-ing the concerns of the project's trustees, who have lately sought to integrate into the structure their longstanding commitment to the natural environment. One of the first of these projects was by R. Buckminster Fuller, who in 1978 suggested a biosphere over the intersection of nave and transept. In 1979 David Sellers suggested developing the unbuilt south transept as a bioshelter. In 1991 the idea for a bioshelter was again taken up by the dean of the cathedral, J.P. Morton, who asked for a "bio-shelter—the first of its kind in the world . . . a new marriage of architecture and material systems that is destined to become the norm for the 21st century . . . in a Gothic cathedral."

Calatrava did not restrict his design to the bioshelter. Considering the building as a whole, he suggested completing the north transept by designing new granite and limestone pillars for the existing plinths and developing an entirely new structural system for the south transept. The original spatial arrangement of the cathedral was reinterpreted while the bioshelter was relocated to the roof space, open to the sky. A lightweight construction was thus created where each triangular panel could rotate about the normal axis to allow the roof to open while preserving its overall shape and allowing rain, light, and air to enter directly into the garden. This aerial greenhouse became part of the cathedral's climate control system, with fresh air generated in the roof space drawn down into the nave and crypt. The bioshelter garden also provides visitors with views of the city.

Views of model

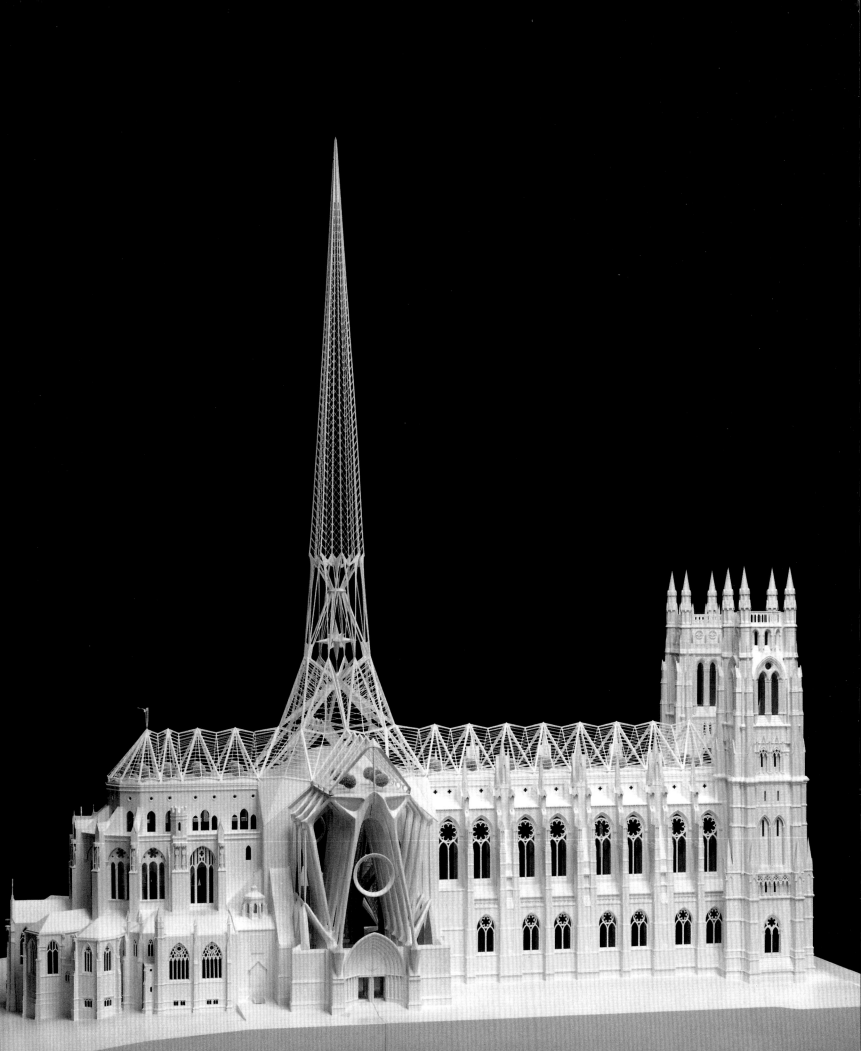

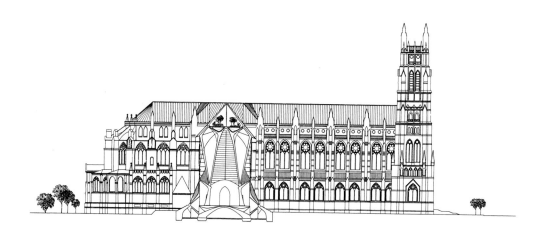

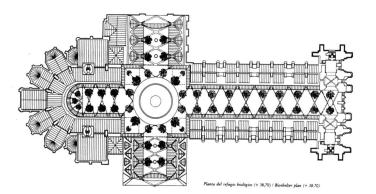

Planta del refugio biológico (+ 38,70) / Bioshelter plan (+ 38.70)

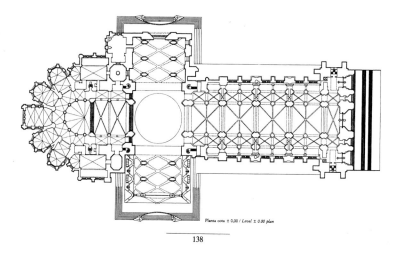

Planta cota ± 0,00 / Level ± 0.00 plan

138

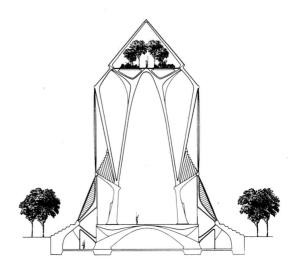

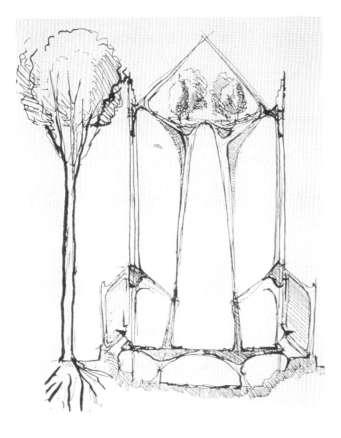

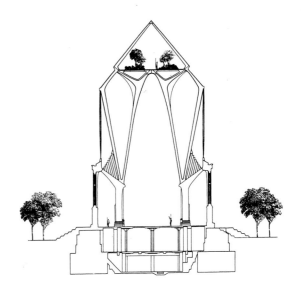

This page: Drawing by
Calatrava (left); sections
(right). Opposite: Section
(top); plan of bioshelter
(center); plan of cathe-
dral (bottom)

The project for Spandau Station, Berlin, Germany, was conceived for a competition, and Calatrava's winning proposal once more went far beyond a mere station complex to suggest an overall urban solution. The design reestablished the continuity between the old parts of Spandau and Wilhelmstadt, close to the banks of the Havel River. The park was extended through the site, passing under the tracks so that the station effectively created a bridge. The roofing for the station employed a new motif for Calatrava, rows of trees on the top of the roof, a filigreed lightweight steel and glass structure. The station area was defined by two ten-story commercial blocks (185 by 45 meters) that straddled the railway, with a total floor space of 40,000 square meters. Below Klosterstrasse is direct access to the subway line from the square, with its public parking and transportation facilities. Following disagreements over a modified and subsequently reduced program, Calatrava withdrew from the project.

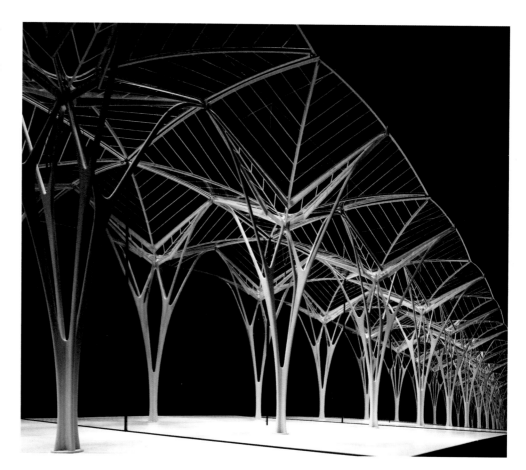

This page: Model of roof. Opposite: View of model showing overall urban plan

The Jahn Olympic Sports Complex, for Berlin, Germany, was part of the city's bid to host the Olympic Games in the year 2000. The brief requested designs for the Olympic boxing hall, the judo hall, and a park. Also included in the project was the development of a housing scheme along the western edge of Mauerpark. Various urban improvements—for example, the layout of Falkplatz and an imposing concept for an entrance at Bernauer and Eberswalder Strasse—were also included. Calatrava's proposal was aimed at reestablishing a spatial presence in the old city. It unites the district with a large park arranged along an axis with dense alignments of trees along the perimeter. The two new structures are placed along the southern edge of the site, preserving the open spaces. The smaller judo hall is placed across the end of the existing sports stadium, which itself is modified to be integrated into the new project through additions, new access points, and a new roof. The two pavilions differ in size but are of a similar character. The project allowed Calatrava the opportunity to employ several building types developed according to his generative principles to create a synthesis of character similar to that achieved by the neoclassicists of nineteenth-century Berlin.

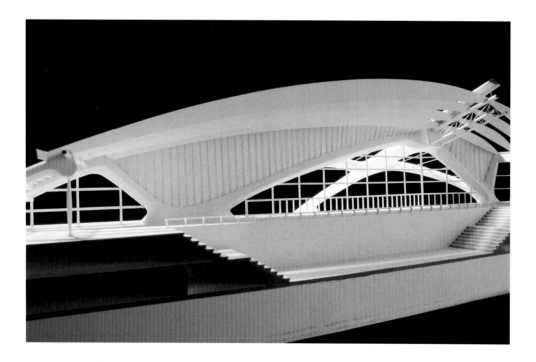

This page: Model showing section of sports hall. Opposite: Model of urban proposal

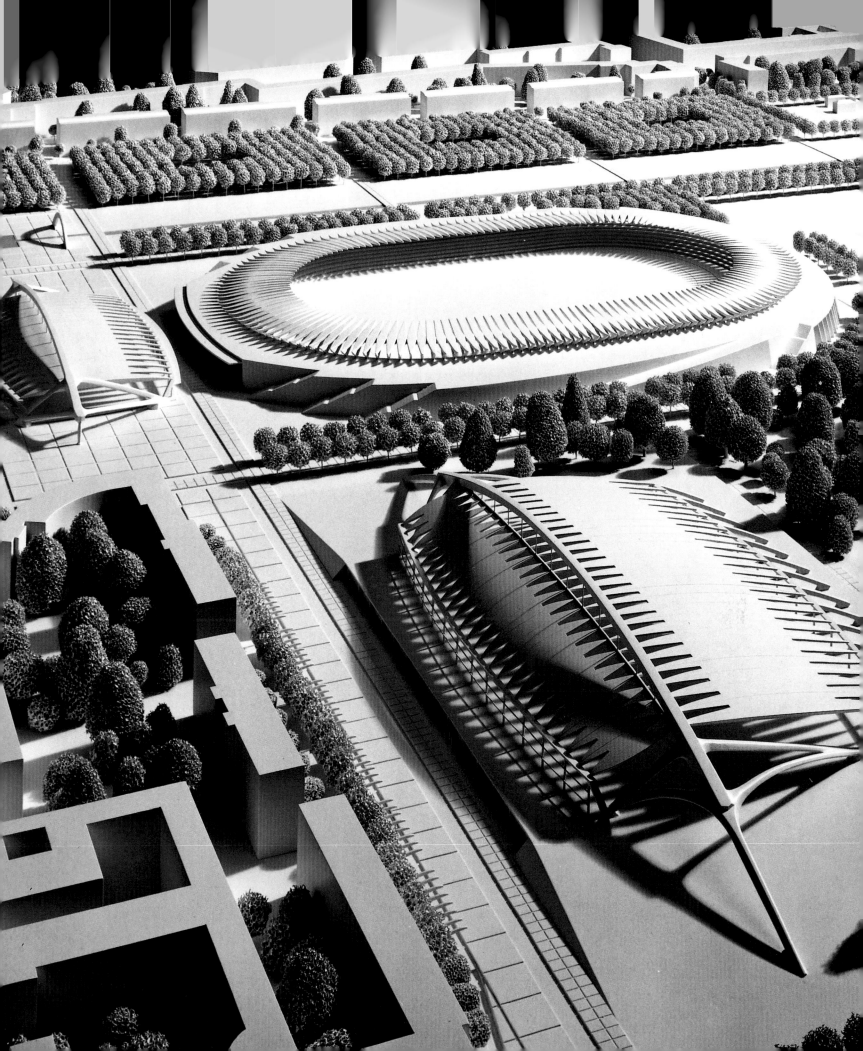

In June 1991 Germany's Bundestag decided to relocate from Bonn to the Reichstag, its former seat in Berlin. The building, intended to unify a fragmented German state, was designed by Paul Wallot, winner of the second Reichstag competition, and was built between 1884 and 1894. It was extensively damaged in 1933 by Nazi arson and again by bombing during World War II. After limited renovation by Paul Baumgarten in 1960 it housed the Berlin state senate and subsequently served as an exhibition and convention center. In June 1992 a single-stage competition was organized for its conversion to house the German Bundestag. Calatrava's entry was one of the three winning proposals, and once again he went beyond what the brief demanded and included an analysis of the urban context, redefining the area between the Spree River to the north and the Brandenburg Gate. He reestablished the building as a freestanding structure, a status it was deprived of by the building of the Berlin Wall during the Cold War. The classicist character of the building was preserved by emphasizing its tripartite spatial organization and its formal relationship to the Brandenburg Gate. Direct access to the heart of the Reichstag was achieved through an underground glazed gallery.

For the Reichstag itself, Calatrava redefined the interior spaces by removing modifications introduced in the 1960s, revealing the characteristic features of the original structure. Where appropriate, the massive walls are made visible, forming a framework to receive the new assembly hall, assembly rooms, and public spaces. The assembly hall is located at ground level, in the central core of the neoclassical building at the intersection of the two major axes, and is bordered by the internal walls of the original structure.

Triangulated steel trusses are braced off the original masonry walls to span the two vaulted, enclosed courtyards, which were thereby transformed into lofty atria. A filigree structural system transfers roof loads to the ground via sculptural pillars. The slender supports carry the loads to the ground and define the interior space. Glazed roofs draw light down into otherwise dark spaces.

The concept of a dome that opens and closes was the most important characteristic of the proposal. Presented during the second phase of the competition, the dome is composed of four three-dimensional segments conceived as curved glass surfaces. An ingenious system of cables acts as a bracing structure and carries the glazed exterior skin. Because cables are tensioned elements, dimensions could be minimized, thus giving the dome a filigree appearance. Calatrava's concept for the dome emerged from the dichotomies of past and future—one might even say from a representation of the tensions of a historically pregnant moment. It transcends the original facade, yet also respects it.

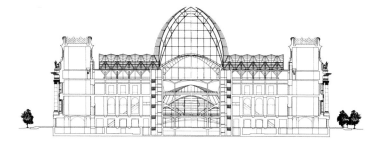

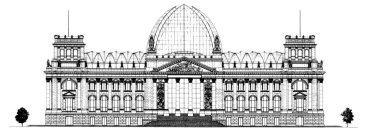

This page: Section and elevation. Opposite: Model showing new structure

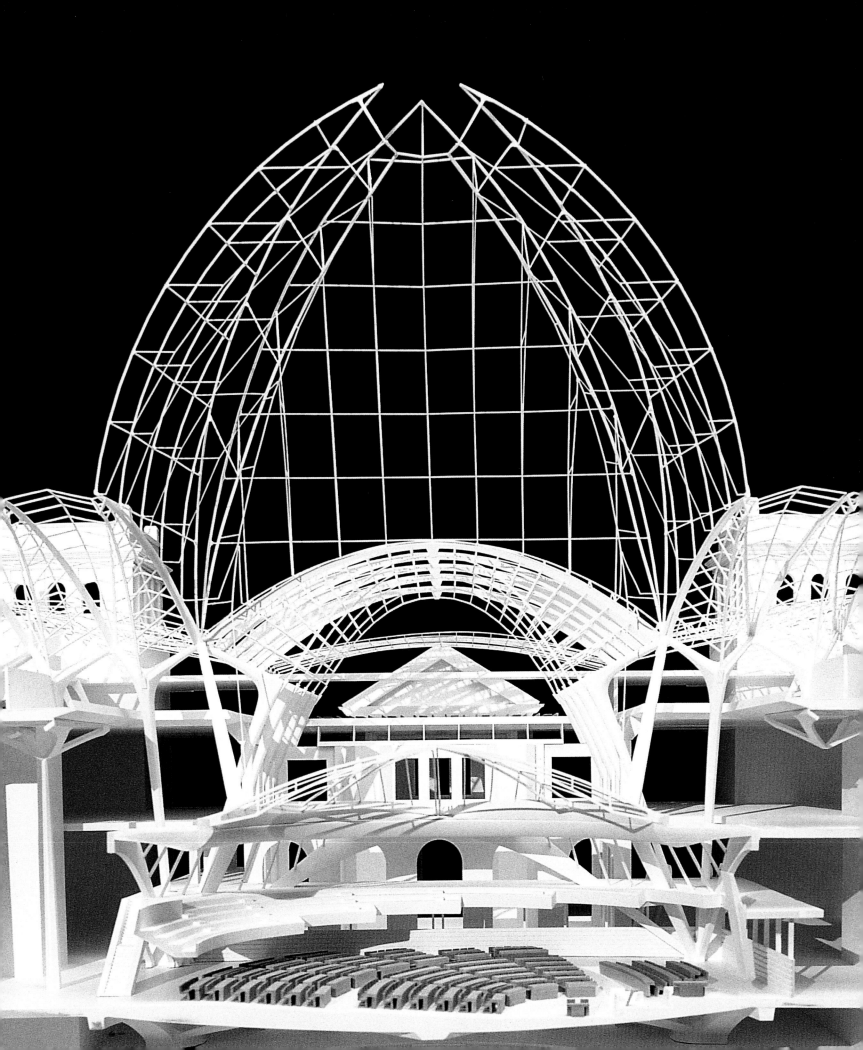

In 1992 Calatrava was commissioned to remodel the central square in the Spanish town of Alcoy, the Plaza de España, a place with a strong historical identity used traditionally for festivals and community events. The commission also included the construction of the Alcoy Community Hall to complement the Santa Maria Church and the town hall as a subterranean multipurpose public space for cultural and social events of all kinds, including exhibitions.

The hall is accessed at either end of the plaza, which is paved with alternating granite slabs and glass panels. The western entrance is set below grade and protected by a stainless steel, pentagonal grid of slats, which are flush with the plaza surface when closed. When raised, the gridlike door structure forms a rectangle, which sculpturally defines the entrance cavity and reveals the stairs. At the east end of the plaza, by the church, the entrance is marked by a fountain in a circular pool. Because festivities can attract large gatherings, the pool features a mechanical cover composed of a metal grid that can be closed to form a secure surface for pedestrians. The entrance here leads down beneath the basin of the pool and into the hall.

The hall has a capacity for six hundred and also provides service and storage facilities. The trapezoidal hall is 90 meters long and 9 meters high, and ranges between 7 and 16 meters wide. The primary support structure of the roof is a concrete arch system, which at the hall's narrowest point bridges the space through a single span. The curve of this arch is repeated throughout the space, transformed to adapt to the increasing width of the hall. The brief of Calatrava's office describes the reasons for this transformation: "Because the springing points must straddle the increasing width, the directrix of the unresolved, symmetrical arch pairs creates a correspondingly marked valley along the longitudinal axis, which in turn cradles a longitudinal supporting arch springing from the east end." The resulting transformational geometry of the structure indicates navigation inside a continuously unfolding space, but also alludes to the dreamy feeling of flight inside a late Baroque building, as well as to a cathedral with strong medieval cathedral undertones, or even the belly of Jonah's whale. Yet, both the technology and geometry is solid and contemporary. The role of lighting was studied very carefully to enhance the sense of movement and airiness. Translucent glass panels mounted in stainless steel frames were inserted between the ribs, letting daylight into the hall while emphasizing the rhythm of the structure. When the hall is used at night the reverse happens: a gentle glow emanates from below.

Stainless steel folding
fountain

This page: Fountain in operation (above); folding entrance in operation (below). Opposite: View of Plaza de España

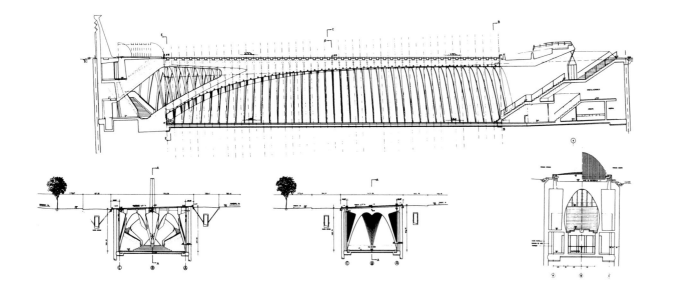

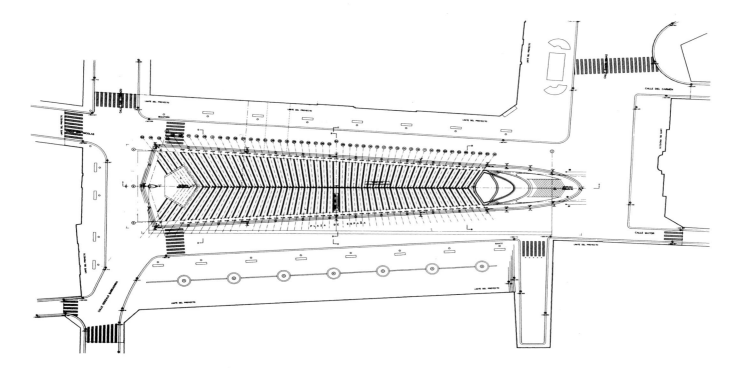

This page: Sections and plan. Opposite: View of underground hall

A midair suspension of objects is suggested by the Trinity Footbridge project, Salford, England. Here Calatrava returns to his long pursued motif of the leaning pylon and the "pregnant moment." The project was intended to mark the first phase of the development of the city's former docklands. As was the first foot crossing linking the adjoining cities of Salford and Manchester, the project signals a return of the site to pedestrian traffic.

The shape of the 41-meter-long pylon recalls the upright structure of the Collserola Telecommunications Tower. The span of the deck suspended from the pylon is 54 meters, bridging the bank's height. Although no S-shaped elements are visible in the configuration of the project, the idea of the contrapposto principle of well-tempered counterpoising forces is implicit.

The bridge took its name from the nearby church, and, interestingly, a triad of constituent elements make up the structure: the pylon, the deck, and the suspending strings connecting the two, creating a transformed hyperbolic paraboloid surface (transformed because the second line is a curve). For Gaudí, the hyperbolic paraboloid surface, with its triadic constitution (generated by a line connecting two lines not on the same surface), symbolized the Holy Trinity, suggesting an homage to the great Catalan master so admired by Calatrava.

General view of bridge
and its context

Sondica Airport Control Tower Bilbao, Spain

The new Sondica Airport Control Tower, part of Bilbao's efforts to modernize, consists of three parts: a symmetrical ramped base, a mast, and the control deck. The base has inclined frontal glazing and contains technical facilities in one wing and administrative offices in the other. The mast, in a teardrop plan, expands toward its top while rising to a height of 42 meters. The control deck (which also is a truncated and inverted cone) has a wraparound observation gallery, which provides access to the tower's mechanical and electronic systems. The basic structure is concrete. A series of steel profiles supports the roof around its periphery. The structure is covered by vertically fluted aluminum cladding hung on an intermediate structure. Despite its upright pose and the circumscribed outline of its figure, movement dominates the tower's scheme. The streamlining of its profile is shaped as if through the process of organic growth over long periods of time like the evolution of birds' wings, or even like the historical evolution of the wing of the jets landing and taking off under the tower's watchful eye.

View of control tower

Chapter 5 | Spinozian Sculptures

When Calatrava presents his work, in proposing ideas to a client, in his lectures, or in exhibitions, he includes along with sketches and images of architectural or engineering projects, almost as a rule, sculptures. The questions raised about Calatrava's commitment in the past to his dissertation research and his continuous work in the notebooks can also be asked about his dedication to sculpture: Why should such an accomplished and prolific designer of buildings, bridges, and even furniture, as we will see, devote time to making sculptures? Is he so taxed by the process of conceiving and constructing complex projects that he needs to escape into the adventure or gentleness of another art, like a warrior coming back to cultivate his garden, or like Ingres finding comfort in his violin? Or is it, as with the dissertation and the notebooks, a way to engage other means of expression to simulate, generate, and test new configurations and new kinds of structure as potential solutions for future buildings and infrastructure projects? I

have long believed that the latter was the case. Sculpture for Calatrava was a domain where he could build models, conceptually and physically, before realizing them as built works. Throughout the chronology of his works, several sculptural studies have preceded and supplied conceptual resources for the design of buildings and bridges. This is clearly the case of the Malmö Turning Torso Tower in Sweden, which will be discussed in detail in the next chapter. In the original versions of the sculpture a series of cubes are set around a steel support to produce a spiral configuration that resembles a twisting human spine. The building's spiraling tower is composed of box units, each containing five floors. The sculpture's steel support is thus translated as the tower's internal nucleus of elevators and stairs through which the apartment units interconnect. And we have already seen a page from the notebooks where the mental leap of transferring by analogy the structure of the body to an object that became a sculpture is doc-

umented more than a decade before the Turning Torso Tower. However, despite this kind of evidence, I now believe Calatrava is not treating sculpture as a handmaid of architecture and engineering, although occasionally he does as an afterthought. Normally his involvement with sculpture is on the same level as the rest of his design activities, as painting was for Le Corbusier during the latest period of his life, or in the tradition of Phidias and Michelangelo, to use even more elevated examples.

In assembling the cubic units and attaching them to a slim metallic frame, Calatrava did not have apartments in mind. His investigation was sculptural, in the sense that he was not contemplating the possibility of inhabiting this object with uses and users. In other words, in designing this sculpture, the world of Calatrava's inquiry was reduced to the exploration of the relationship between the process of rotation with the pure, solid cubes and the set of precise nets of dense, thin sticks, in short, with movement and structure.

Twisted Spine sculpture

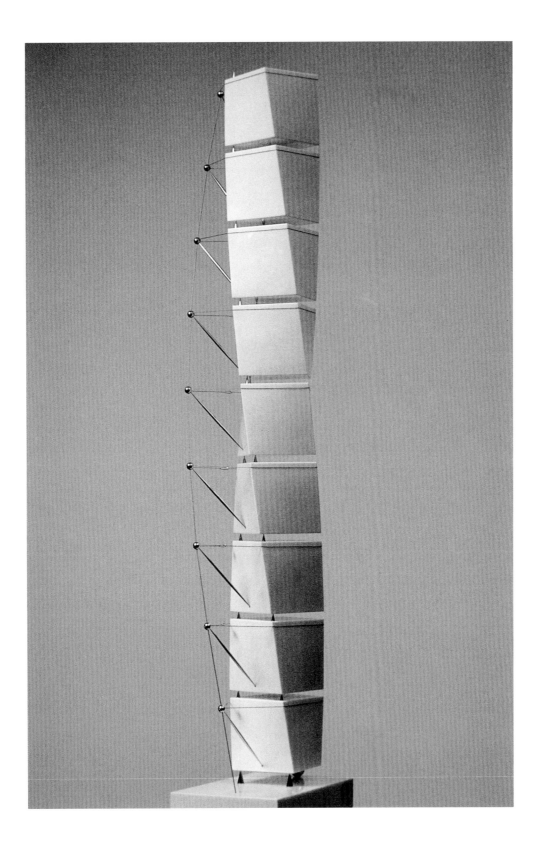

In many respects Caltrava's sculptures are reminiscent of the paintings of Kasimir Malevich during his later period, or rather Malevich's approach to painting. Like Malevich's paintings, precision is part of their nature and their materials are irrelevant. And as, closer to our time, Ad Reinhardt's later paintings as well as Anthony Caro and Donald Judd's sculptures, Calatrava's sculptures are neither representations nor compositions. As Michael Levin has remarked, Calatrava's sculpture cannot be characterized as intentionally referential in the postmodernist sense.[1] Calatrava's sculptures are constructions, but not in the manner of Malevich's work and the works of the "minimalists" mentioned above, which, according to Judd, writing in the March/May 1968 issue of *Perspecta*, are "matters of fact . . . just arrangements." Calatrava's intentions are "minimalist maximal." As construc-

tions, they achieve "order or disorder in general" by including both movement *and* structure—they incorporate movement *in* structure.[2]

Like Bach's variations they are constructed gradually through operations of transformation augmenting the number of elements and their various relationships, increasing their complexity: from a single box suspended in front of a single straight pole, to a box supported by one inclined pole and suspended between two inclined poles, to a series of boxes cantilevered through tensioned strings from an inclined pole. Common to all these objects is that they follow each other in a sort of combinatorial way to offer a cognitive-aesthetic experience richer than the more cerebral experience offered by the series of folding structures in the dissertation.

Also common to these objects is that they are "pregnant" with movement. They are struc-

tures that appear nascent and on the brink of falling at the same time. Like Bach's *Art of the Fugue*, they present a controlled but open-ended set of parts and connections, emerging and disappearing, as preludes and fugues unfold and fade away.

As I describe these sculptures, I might give the impression that in order to comprehend, appreciate, and enjoy them, one has to pore over them all at once as pieces that belong to a series rather than looking at them as works in isolation. Without diminishing the unique delight of grasping them as a group I will argue that one of the deep delights of studying any of them independently is the potential of each one to appear as an example of a type, suggesting multiple alternative combinations. In other words one can see, suggested through the individual sculpture, the group.

Sculpture studies with cubes

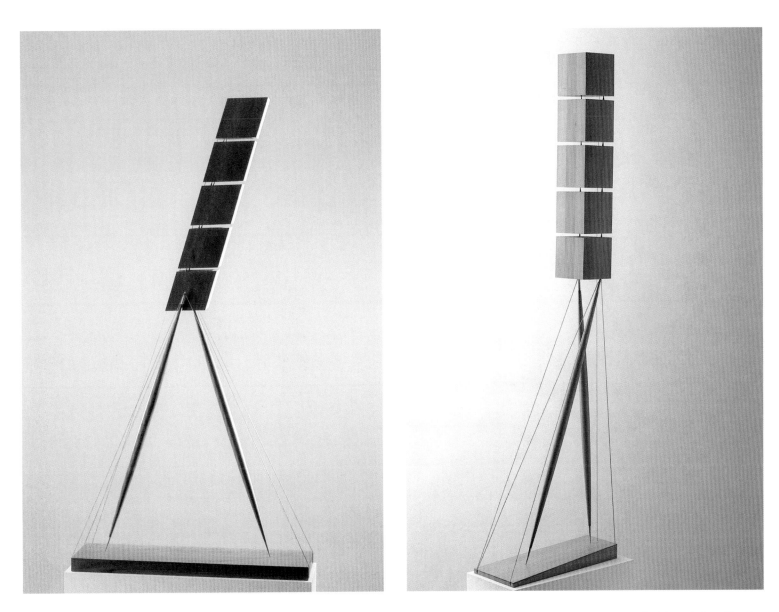

Sculpture studies with cubes

| Aegean Cycle and Stage Setting for *Ecuba*

Calatrava created a series of sculptures referred to as the "Aegean Cycle," and in the purity, simplicity, and pregnancy of the form of each work one can discern the group. One can also perceive how each piece is derived from a single prototypical form. Generic movement is involved in carrying out these implied transformations and in the subtle operations of the three-dimensional compasses that construct the curves of the sculptures' forms in a manner similar to the performance of folding structures as compasses. A similar approach was adopted in the stage setting for a production of *Ecuba* and in several other sculptures for which only a single prototype was designed.

This page: Model of stage setting for *Ecuba*. Opposite: "Aegean Cycle" series

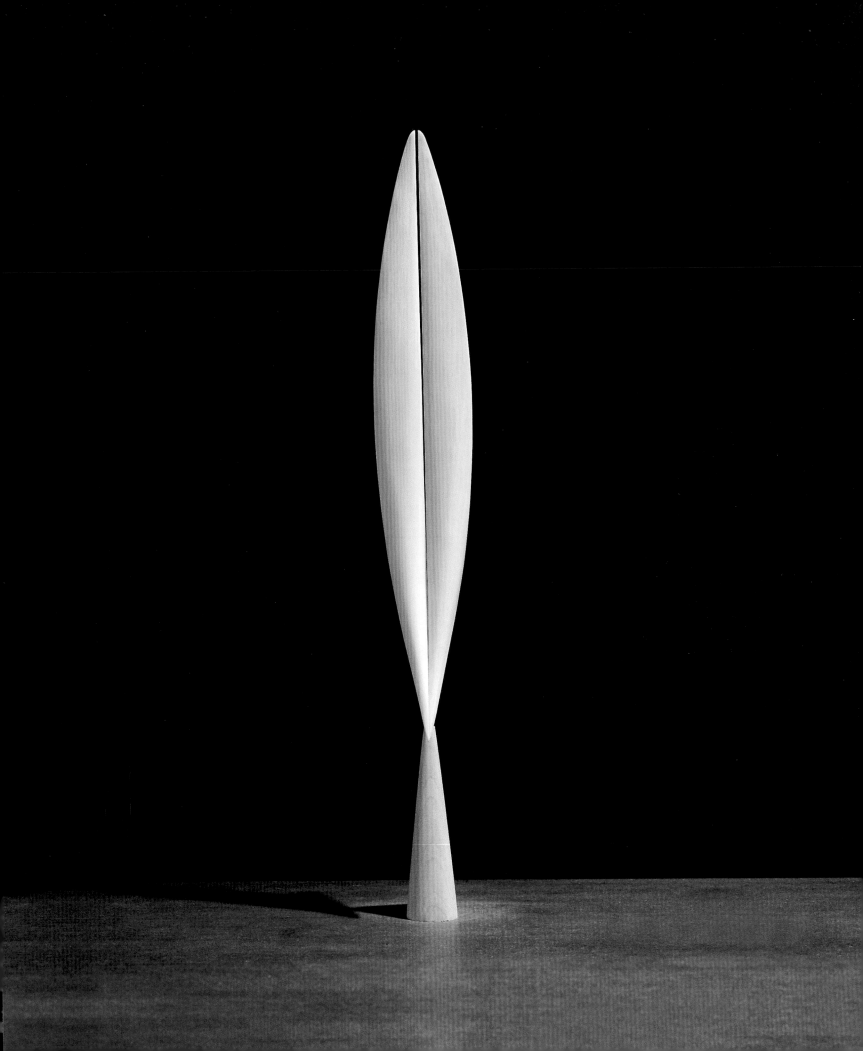

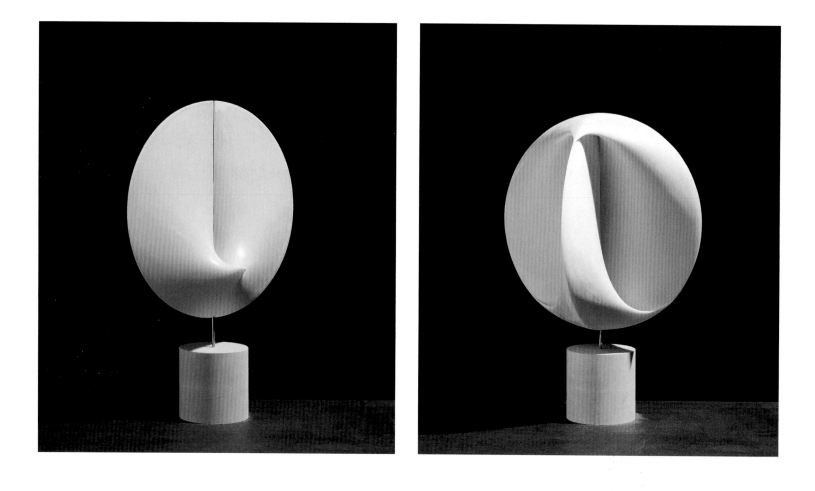

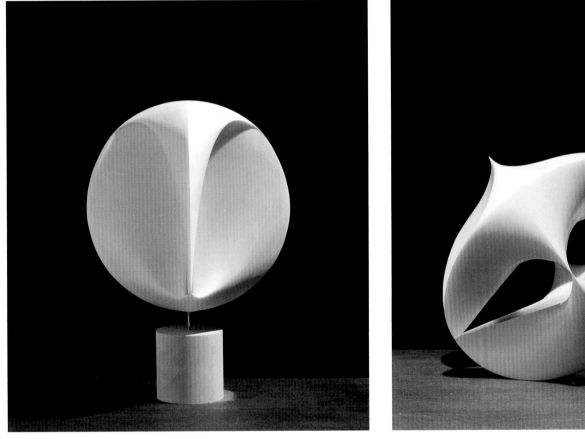

"Aegean Cycle" series

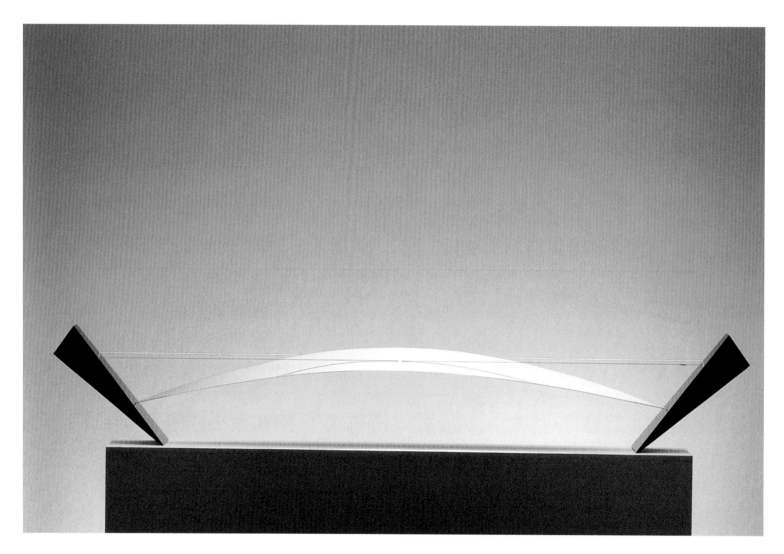

Golden Bridge sculpture

Golden Leaf sculpture

This page: *Eye* or
Pecking Bird sculpture.
Opposite: *Palmette*.
Overleaf: *Curving Spine*
sculpture

In 1999 Calatrava produced the winning design for a time capsule competition organized by the *New York Times* to celebrate the millennium. The capsule, on permanent display at the American Museum of Natural History in New York City, was intended to be a repository of twentieth-century civilization to be opened in a thousand years. The design was based on the combinations of the line, circle, and square, recalling the anthropomorphic elementarism of Leonardo and Le Corbusier. In the capsule, the generation and evolution of several examples out of one type-object is explicit. The capsule's various components are movable, and by physically unfolding it in stages one can see at each stage an example of the generic group-type.

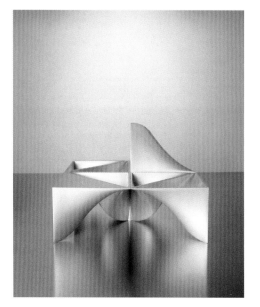
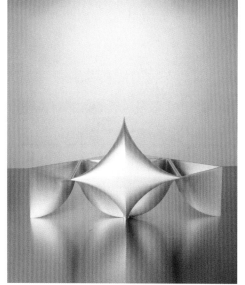
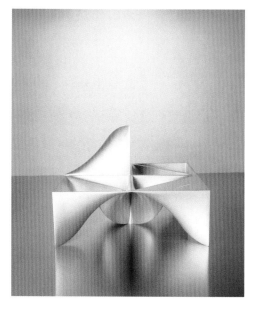

Views of *Times Capsule*

In some of Calatrava's sculptures the presence of movement is explicit, physical, and mechanized. Calatrava experimented with this directness in several "toy models" before finally applying it to a built work in the Swissbau Pavilion, an exhibition stand of mobile concrete elements for the 1988 Swiss Building Fair in Basel, Switzerland. The Swiss Association of Manufacturers of Precast Cement Elements commissioned Calatrava to develop an innovative structure that would demonstrate modern concrete casting technology at the experimental level. Calatrava challenged the fixed spatial image of rigid concrete as a static material for construction by putting it in motion. He also challenged the manufacturers by exploring the engineering problems associated with casting high-strength, dynamically loaded concrete, using oiled, linoleum-lined, compound-curve precision formwork. To achieve a very compact, fine-grained, silky finish, careful consideration of steel reinforcement and meticulous temperature control during the curing process were required. Each of the fourteen individually cast elements of this articulated "rib cage" are 7.8 meters long, between 10 and 52 centimeters in width, and weigh 1.2 tons.

Balanced on trunnions that rest on concrete brackets cantilevered 1.86 meters from the rear support wall, these graceful aerodynamic ribs connect via a series of cranks to a row of eccentric pins, which in turn connect at progressively staggered angles to an endless chain. This drive configuration produces a cyclic wave motion in the slender tips extending above the floor. The elements that compose the object thus adopt a rhythm, with the periodic slow motion of the roof creating a rolling, volumetric change in the space below.

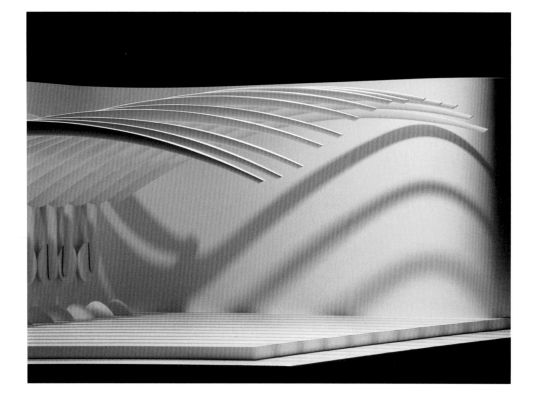

This page: View of model. Opposite: Built exhibition stand

Calatrava's idea of moving sculptures was advanced in *Shadow Machine* (1992). The sculpture was commissioned by a private client in Switzerland to coincide with the solo exhibition of Calatrava's work at the Museum of Modern Art in New York City. Twelve slender "fingers"—long pointed elements attached on a joint on one end and free on the other so as to be able to move around, as in an earlier sculpture—were constructed out of molded precast concrete elements, each 8 meters long and weighing 600 kilograms, and mounted on a rear support panel. Naturally tinted through the use of white sand in the aggregate, the concrete elements were supported from a base weighing 30 tons, which was lifted as one piece over the wall of the museum's Abby Aldrich Rockefeller Sculpture Garden. A socket cast into each finger engaged a ball, which was set into the end of the protruding supports. This ball-and-socket structure allowed each finger to have fully articulated motion, powered by eccentric drives mounted on the rear panel. A progressive change in the angle of engagement with an endless chain produced a staggered, synchronized motion. Due to the direct connection between the finger and the eccentric drive socket, the full circular motion of the drive was transmitted to the tips. Later the machine was moved to Venice, Italy, where it was exhibited for a period under the curious name *Icaros*.

A similar kind of movement appears in two other sculptures by Calatrava. Let us call them *Wave* and *Weed*. They both involve a rather simple rotation mechanism translated into a visible oscillation pattern that suggests the effect of the wind, either blowing over a liquid body, causing it to swell, surge, and propagate in space, or over long-stemmed reeds, making them waver gently. Both *Wave* and *Weed* are products of representation and construction. They bring to mind the response of the great Russian-born sculptor Naum Gabo to Herbert Read's reductive claims that his works were "anti-realist." "I get my forms," Gabo declared, "[from] everywhere around me . . . in a torn piece carried away by the wind . . . the green thicket of leaves and trees . . . in a steamy trail of smoke [and shape them into] any thing or action which enhances life, propels it, and adds to it."[3]

This page: Early sculpture showing "finger" principle. Opposite: *Shadow Machine* at the Museum of Modern Art, New York City. Overleaf: *Icaros* installed in Venice, Italy

As in Calatrava's other sculptures, the geometry, the materials, the motion, and the mechanism of *Shadow Machine*, *Wave*, and *Weed* are impeccable, maintaining all the attributes of a high-quality technical work. For sculpture, however, such attributes carry the risk that the work will become, to use Clement Greenberg's term, "Good Design." But Calatrava manages to avoid this pitfall. To start with there is an aura of Oldenburg and Buñuel in *Shadow Machine*, *Wave*, and *Weed*, intelligence fused with oxymoron. As opposed to Good Design, Calatrava makes design that is good, that is rigorous and moral, as Good Design is not. The rigor of his constructions brings to mind Spinoza: "I shall consider human actions and desires . . . as though I were concerned with lines, planes, and solids . . . I should attempt to treat of human vice and folly geometrically."[4]

For Spinoza geometry did not imprison the world but liberated it from the idolatry of dogma, no matter how perfect dogma appeared to be. For Calatrava, too, the geometrical precision of his works does not necessarily indicate a finished state. In fact the exactness of their geometry makes them resemble Michelangelo's "*non finito*," unfinished sculptures expressed in form and surface as figures barely emerging from the mass of the unworked rough stone, "growing larger as the stone grows small," as Michelangelo himself described in his poem "*Sicome per levar*."[5]

In Calatrava's case, the openness of his process is manifested in the movement incorporated in his structures, which makes them appear perpetually suspended between coming together and falling apart. As Swiss psychologist Jean Piaget has observed, children in the most intensive stage of learning, rather than putting together structures, appear to indulge in their destruction, throwing them down and taking them apart. They interpret the world not as a static thing but as a construct of open promises. And it is here, at this particular epistemological and moral junction, where Calatrava's work in sculpture, architecture, and engineering come together in the shared task of making the world into a universe of open possibilities.

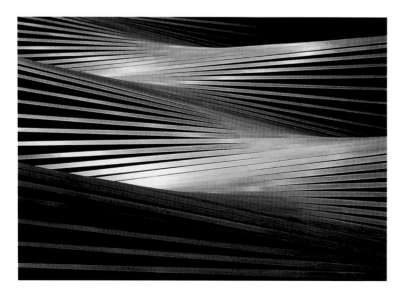

This page: *Wave* sculpture. Opposite: *Weed* sculpture

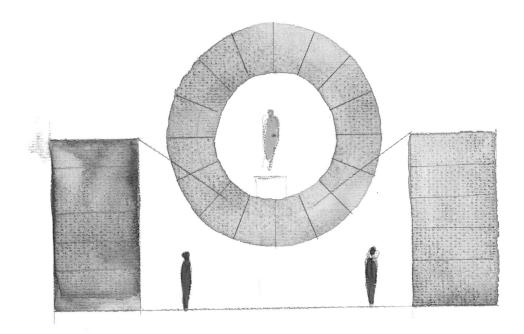

Drawings of suspended
objects by Calatrava

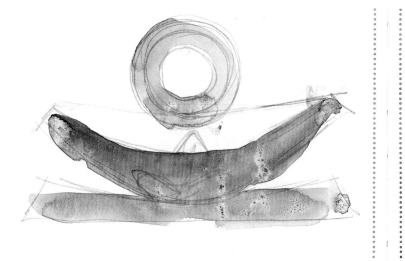

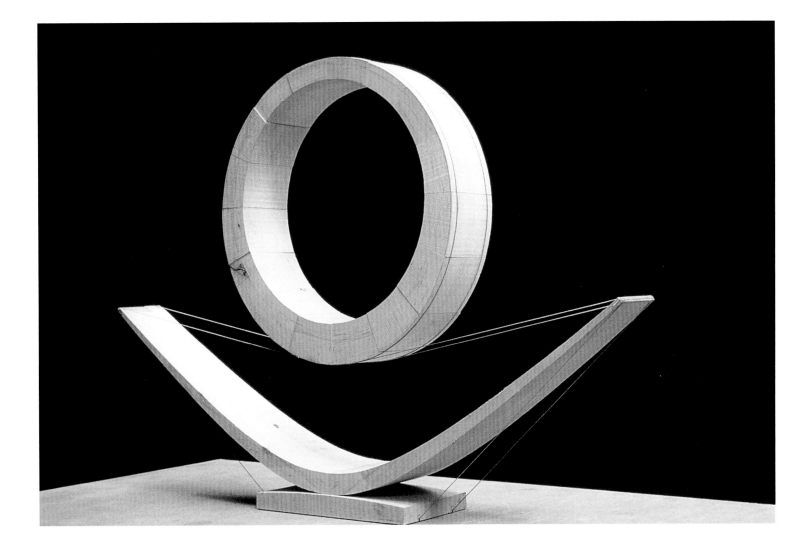

This page: *Suspended
Object* or *Discerning Eye*
sculpture. Opposite:
Drawings of suspended
objects by Calatrava

Chapter 6 | Landmarking

The 1990s were a period of consolidation and synthesis, for Calatrava, who took the opportunity to develop and recombine nascent and tested themes in a series of larger-scale projects. Oriente Station, the transportation hub for the northeast district of Lisbon, Portugal, provided a major opportunity to develop earlier motifs and findings. Again, the project was the result of an invited competition, which Calatrava won in 1993. The station was intended to be the primary transportation connection for the 1998 World's Fair that Portugal was to host in the Olivais district, some five kilometers from the heart of Lisbon. Located between the railway and a river embankment, the area was an industrial wasteland at the time of the competition to be completely renewed after the fair ended. The planners and city officials intended the station to become not only the main component in the transformation of the whole area but also one of Europe's most comprehensive transport interchanges to encompass high-speed intercity trains, rapid regional transport, standard rail services, and tram and metro networks.

Responding to the challenge, Calatrava, once more appealed to the ambitions of the planning committee, going beyond the strict requirements of the competition to propose a comprehensive urban plan. Thus, in addition to the scheme for a new station on the existing railway lines—which crossed the district on the embankment defining the western edge of the fair's site, historically a dividing line between residential and industrial areas—Calatrava suggested a plan that pierced the embankment and linked it to the Olivais district. Such a strategy would have the added advantage of making the various transport modes accessible to pedestrian traffic, and to realize this the decision was made to elevate the station and to locate it to the north of the designated site.

Compared to Stadelhofen Railway Station in Zurich and the Lyons Airport Station, the organization of Oriente Station is much more complex in its use of levels. The train platforms of the station are located on a bridge structure comprising five parallel rows of twinned arches 78 meters in total width and spanning 260 meters. The bus terminal is located immediately to the west of the station, and a complex of commercial buildings is arranged around a piazza to the east with access to a shopping mall and ticket counters within a multilevel hall directly beneath the platforms. A park-and-ride facility and metro link are placed below grade. The bus terminal consists of a series of glazed canopies that lead to an elevated gallery that runs through the entire complex from west to east and connects to the station above the bus lanes. A decade later Calatrava proposed an expanded version of this canopy for the Nuova Stazione in Florence.

The pragmatic orthogonal arrangement of the plan that weaves the various modes of transportation into one compound contrasts with the canopy-like roof above the platforms, which invites reverie and fantasy. For the roof Calatrava reused the tree motif developed for BCE Place in Toronto and several other structures, applying it here in a 17-meter grid arranged like an orchard. One might read his tree motif here as an homage to the grandiose forests of arched supports found in railway stations of the past such as McKim, Mead & White's Pennsylvania Station in New York City. In fact, Calatrava participated in a competition for the remodeling of the new Pennsylvania Station in 1998, proposing a flamboyant vaulted structure. But in contrast to the proud and sublime aura of Pennsylvania Station, Calatrava created a warm and inviting atmosphere for Oriente Station: the rooftop orchard together with the curvilinear canopies of the bus station, extending like the gigantic leaves of tropical plants, announce departures to calmer worlds to be reached through the magic of movement.

Opposite: View of platforms. Overleaf: Night view of entrance

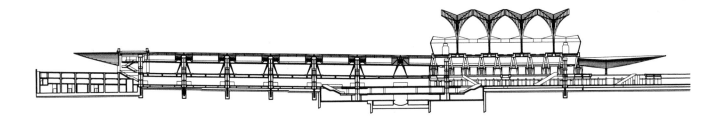

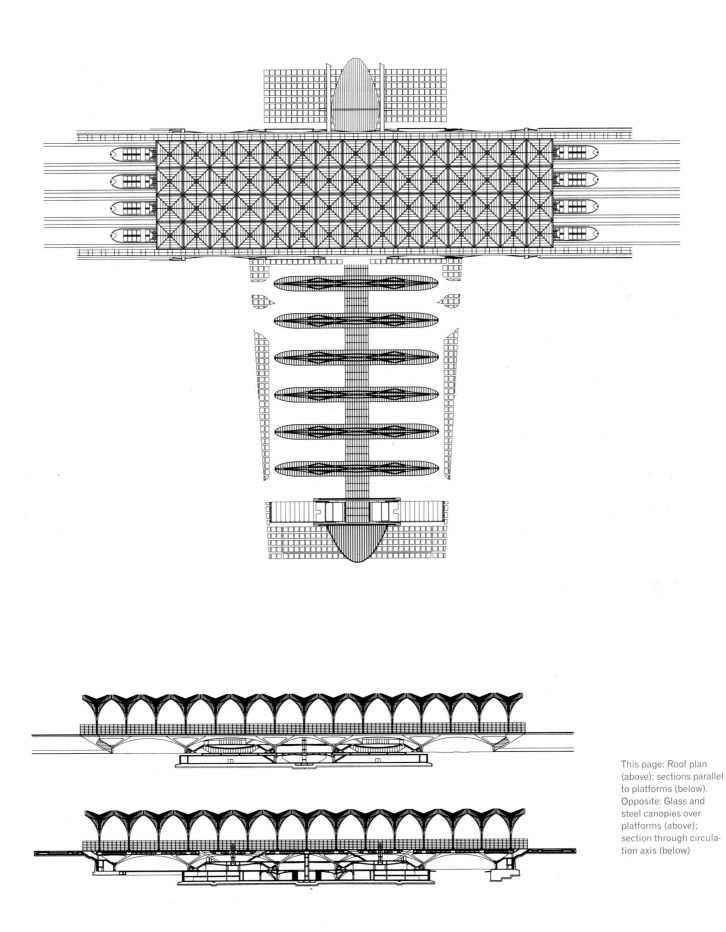

This page: Roof plan (above); sections parallel to platforms (below). Opposite: Glass and steel canopies over platforms (above); section through circulation axis (below)

Image and emotion are ever present in the scheme for the Milwaukee Art Museum. This is the richest and most complex project of the era of recombination and elaborate synthesis of seminal themes that the 1990s represented. The complex expands upon an existing site composed of Eero Saarinen's Metropolitan Milwaukee War Memorial (1940–64) and David Kahler's 1975 exhibition space, which extends to the edge of Lake Michigan, with 160,000 square meters of floor space. Calatrava was invited to participate in a competition asking to design a more accessible and identifiable entrance and an overall scheme that presented a stronger public image, which the museum's trustees thought the previous building was lacking.

Visitors on foot cross Lincoln Memorial Drive to enter the pavilion while those by car enter either from a vaulted underground parking garage or from the main driveway in front of the new entrance. The plan includes an atrium, 1,500 square meters of gallery space for temporary exhibitions, an education center with a 300-seat lecture hall, a gift shop, and a restaurant with commanding panoramic views onto the lake. The plan also permits future expansion.

Calatrava's proposal used certain contextual conditions as points of departure: Calatrava decided to let the existing structure remain intact as a separate entity, conceiving his extension as an autonomous unit; and the new building's proximity to the lake inspired him to use analogies with aquatic objects in the design of basic components for the proposal. The shapes of the structure, and to some degree its color and the materials, such as the use of white steel, remind one of a ship. More importantly, the structure evokes an enormous folding brise-soleil, a spectacular kinetic structure with louvers that open and close, like the wings of a great seagull. The bridge for accessing the museum draws from Calatrava's previous bridge type using a single inclined mast, yet another marine image.

The brise-soleil is made out of steel plates, welded and stiffened inside, and it consists of two wing elements, each formed by thirty-six fins, whose length ranges between 32 and 8 meters, cantilevered from a rotating spine joined by five rows of tying tubular sections. The angles at which each fin meets the rotating spine are all different, so that in its closed position the brise-soleil forms a ruled surface with a conical shape. In its open position, the longest fin remains parallel to the ground plane, so that the wings form a semiparaboloid shape. The mechanical wings, weighing approximately 115 tons, are controlled manually according to exhibition requirements. However, during bad weather, when wind speed is over 40 miles per hour, a computerized system controlled by a wind gauge closes the brise-soleil automatically. The striking formal coincidence of a ship's mast and seabird, stressed by the parallel, 47-degree incline of the two leaning masts—the mast on which the axis of the pivot line for the brise-soleil's slats is based, and the mast of the adjacent bridge—has created one of the most elegant works yet produced by Calatrava's poetics of structure and movement.

Opposite: View of the new entrance to the museum. Overleaf: View of museum against Lake Michigan

This page: Preliminary
sketch by Calatrava.
Opposite: View of
museum complex with
surrounding urban
context

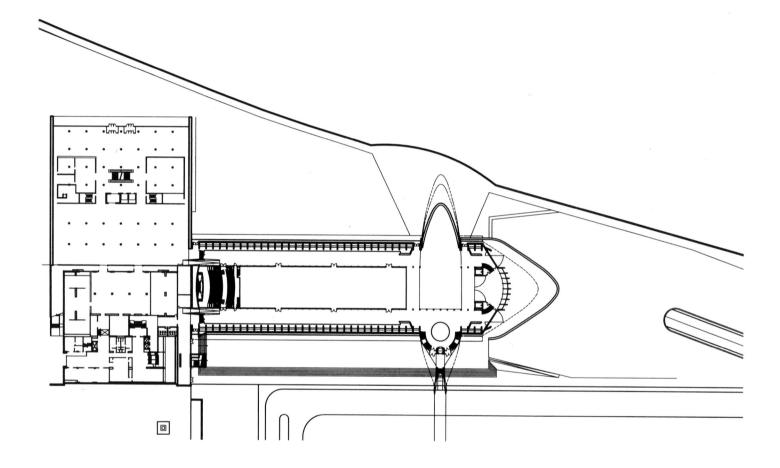

This page: Plan. Opposite: Sections through hall and through new wing

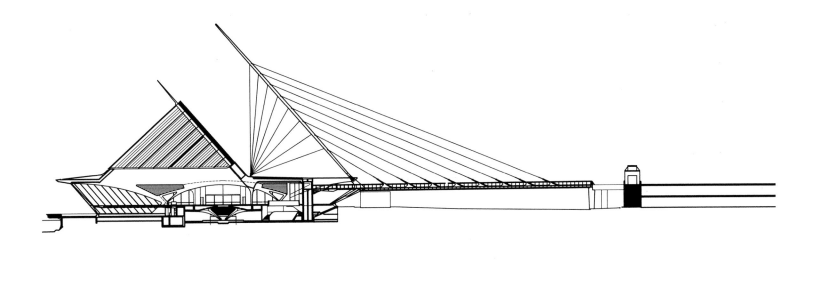

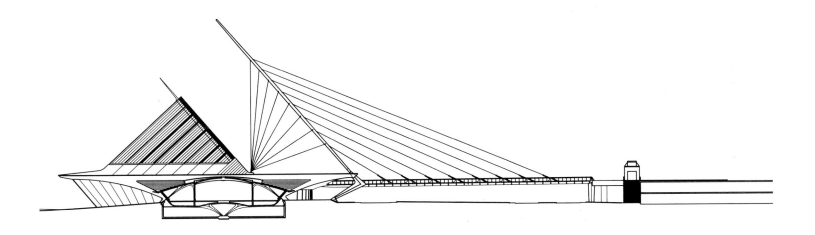

This page: Brise-soleil
in open and closed
positions. Opposite:
View of brise-soleil
in operation

This page: View of
entrance hall. Opposite:
Detail view of ceiling.
Overleaf: View through
corridor

Simultaneous with various complex buildings Calatrava continued to experiment with intricate types of bridges emphasizing extreme alternatives among structures, choosing for each site the type adapting best to the given natural or cultural landscape and advancing it to its most developed solution in built form, as in the Manrique Footbridge, Murcia, Spain (1994–99). One can see the richness of Calatrava's tool kit of types, and the sensitivity and intelligence of their adaptation, in two of the most extreme examples of bridge configurations: the spirited Embankment Renaissance Footbridge, Bedford, England, designed in 1995, with its vertical supports parading in a row across the river; and the Quarto Ponte sul Canal Grande, designed a year later with a quiet, low silhouette for the demanding environment of Venice, Italy.

This page: Embankment Renaissance Footbridge. Opposite: Manrique Footbridge. Overleaf: Quarto Ponte sul Canal Grande

In 1996 Calatrava returned to the theme of the folding structure. After first appearing in the dissertation and notebooks in the 1980s, the strategy achieved built form in the seminal doors of the Ernsting Warehouse in 1983 and further developed in the folding roofs with moving ribs, in projects such as the 1991 Kuwait Pavilion and in the rib-frames of the Reichstag dome in 1992. For the Church of the Year 2000 in Rome, Italy, Calatrava recalled this theme along with another idea seen in an early project, the 1979 IBA Squash Hall structure, where the moving structure assumes by analogy the figure of a winged creature. The project was conceived to mark the Catholic Church Conference of Bishops by creating a structure to symbolically acknowledge the event. Its location in the Tor Tre Teste area on the eastern periphery of Rome was intended to help unify an otherwise fragmented district. On behalf of Pope John Paul II, the Roman Catholic Church organized an invitational competition for the church's design. The six entrants were Tadao Ando, Günter Behnisch, Santiago Calatrava, Peter Eisenman, Frank Gehry, and Richard Meier. Calatrava's proposal for the building, to be constructed on a graded, split-level site, was based on a truncated, elliptical plan and was composed of a concrete shell penetrated by slender, wide-span arches on the lower level. The most significant aspect of the project, however, is the moving roof made of a steeply inclined, thrusting ridge that formed the hinge line for a series of articulated slats. When closed, the slats shield the conical apse. Inside, a series of repeated, pierced-concrete arches rise toward the altar, which is dappled in light from tinted glazing overhead. Framed between the rectory and the main body of the building is an entry foyer providing a covered link to a community hall, auditorium, and catechism chambers on the lower level. Calatrava's proposal was extreme within the given setting and did not win; however, in many respects it perfectly captured the spirit of the event in terms of the explicit symbolism of the "flying" folding structure of the roof as well as in the enthusiastic communal spirit of the project's configuration. In addition, the project was a useful exercise in the course of the evolution of the roof motif that would reach Manhattan almost a decade later.

View of model

In 1996 Calatrava continued to work on the City of Arts and Sciences complex, specifically on the Valencia Opera House (Palau de les Arts), which was completed in 2004. In contrast to the Church of the Year 2000, the project turns inward, like a seashell, guarding the magic of the spectacles performed there. There are two aspects that are particularly captivating: the striking streamline configuration of the volume; and the agility with which the collection of concrete shell structures and the various heterogeneous spaces of the building form one unified enclosing system. The volumes of the building are organized between horizontal promenade decks, which cantilever off the side of the structure. The central core is occupied by the 1,300-seat opera house auditorium, which is set within an acoustical shell embedded within the cluster of structures. The central core also includes the orchestra pit, stage services, and stage mechanisms. A smaller auditorium for chamber music seats 400, while a large auditorium to the east, partially protected beneath the open shell, seats 2,000. Calatrava envisioned events staged simultaneously in the various locations among the volumes. The roof and defining walls enclosing the complex perform an acoustical function for the open performance areas, while a glass-covered, insulated rehearsal area is provided above the chamber music hall.

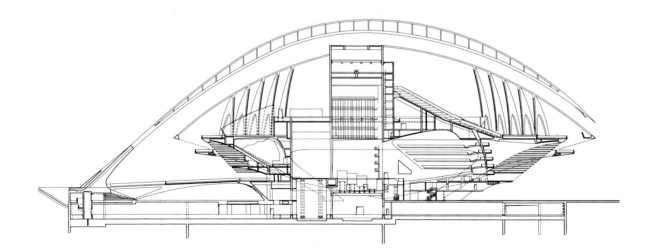

This page: Section.
Opposite: Overall view

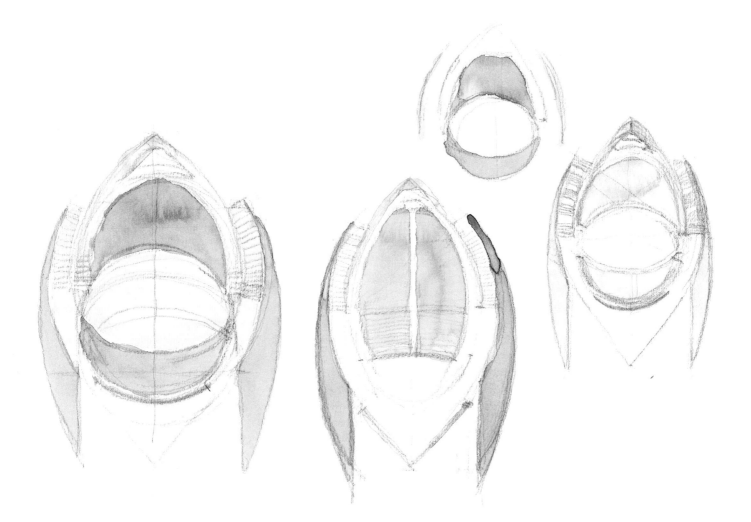

This page: Preliminary
sketches by Calatrava.
Opposite: View of model
with outer shell (above);
sectioned model (below)

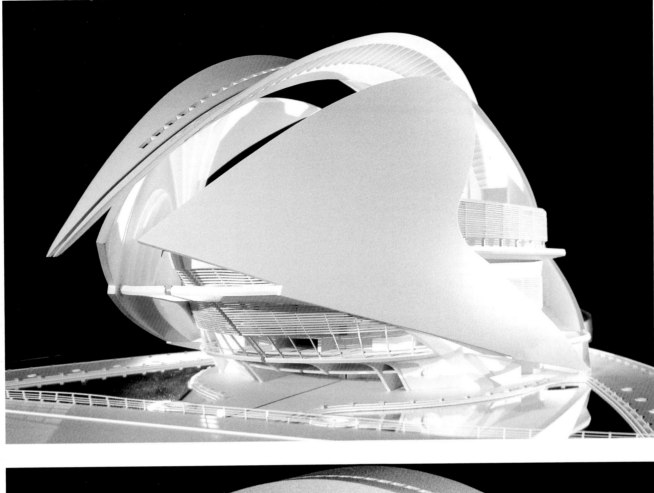

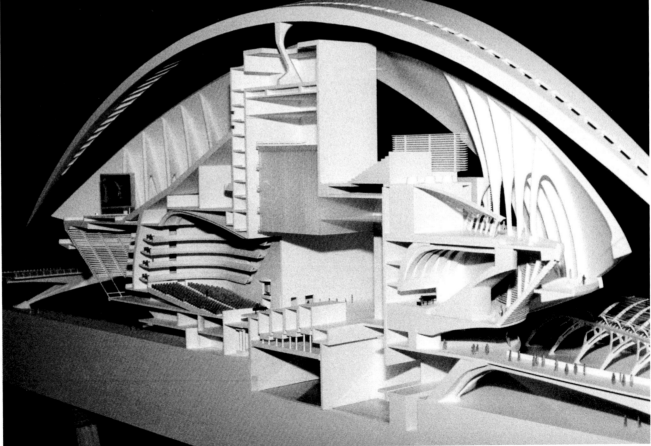

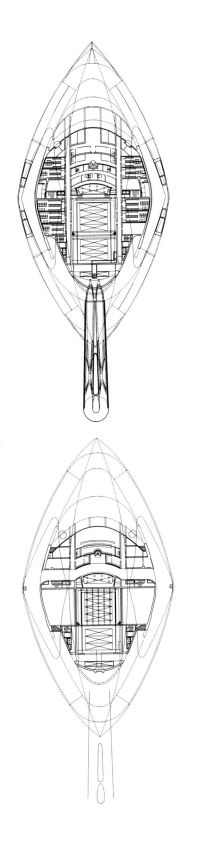

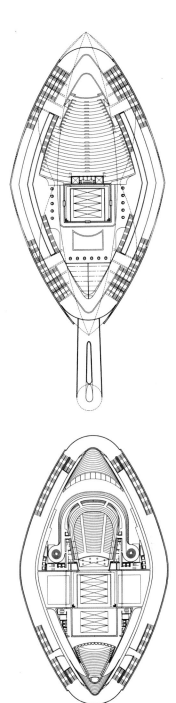

This page: Floor plans.
Opposite: Circulation
space between building
and outer shell

The Pont d'Orléans (Pont de l'Europe), Orléans, France, was designed during the same productive year as several other projects, in 1996. Calatrava won this challenging commission through a competition organized by the consortium of local communities making up the region of Orléans. The bridge was to link the communities of Saint-Jean de la Ruelle to the north and Saint-Pryvé Saint-Mesmin to the south, on either side of the Loire River. The real challenge for Calatrava was not so much the functional requirements as the proximity of the new bridge

to the adored eighteenth-century Pont Royal (Pont George V), which as an extension of the Rue Royale leads to the heart of the local urban concentration—the place where a statue of Joan of Arc stands.

The steel structure for the new bridge has symmetrical piers, cut as modern bastions that recall the Pont Royal and are intended to create a new gateway for the city. The bridge employs a suspended inclined arch standing on clear concrete pylons, with the arch's novel inclination and its color giving the bridge added pres-

ence as an urban gateway. The steel deck is composed of three sections, two 88.2 meters and one 201.6 meters, to give the bridge a total length of 378 meters. The main section is suspended from the decentralized inclined arch by two series of twenty-eight hangers. The buttresses at the lower embankment of the Loire are made of prestressed concrete and give the bridge an overall length of 470.6 meters. The transverse section of the deck is raised, allowing pedestrians a panoramic view of the city and the Loire embankments.

This page: Night view with lighted structure. Opposite: Pedestrians cross under inclined arch. Overleaf: View of bridge with surrounding natural context

1998–2000 | **Pont des Guillemins** Liège, Belgium

For the Pont des Guillemins in Liège, Belgium, Calatrava advanced ideas he first experimented with in the Volantin Footbridge in Bilbao. The span of the Pont des Guillemins is 80 meters while an adjacent viaduct spans 122 meters; its deck is 12 meters wide, and its arch reaches a height of 19.6 meters. As he did with the Bilbao bridge, Calatrava applied a rectilinear torsion tube, to which twenty-five bridge elements are welded, radiating to form the arc of the circle described by the plan of the deck. The arch is made of a steel tube welded at each end to the torsion tube of the deck.

The bridge connects the motorway that crosses Liège to an 800-space parking facility for a new railway station, also designed by Calatrava. Although the bridge serves as an automobile conduit it is also a pedestrian and bicycle link providing a tranquil path and a green space for the residential district at the foot of the Cointe hill district. As in the Volantin Footbridge, the curve of the deck and the tension lines of the tube and vertical projection of the arch create the sense of a structure waiting to unleash potential movement, a dramatic contrast to the serene, nestlike character of the surrounding greenery and buildings.

This page: View of
bridge against hills.
Opposite: View of arch

La Rioja Bodegas Ysios winery complex in La Guardia, Spain, was designed for the Bodegas & Bebidas Group. The scheme for this low-industry facility responded to the need to accommodate basic operations of wine production: to make, store, and sell wine. But it also addressed the client's desire for an iconic structure to function as a kind of trademark for its prestigious new wine. Located in the Rioja wine growing region of Spain, about an hour south of Bilbao by car, Ysios is one of the first Spanish wineries to compete with their French counterparts to the north. The building is located in a roughly rectangular site, with pronounced grade changes, half of which is covered with vineyards. The building's 8,000-square-meter plan has a simple linear configuration to accommodate the winemaking process and is placed along an east-west axis. It is constructed by two longitudinal concrete load-bearing walls, 26 meters apart and 196 meters long, with a sinusoidal shape in plan and in elevation. The walls are clad with wooden planks. In a manner consistent with the facade, the roof is composed of a longitudinal series of laminated wood beams supported on the staggered sinusoidal cornice of the lateral walls. In contrast to the warmth of the wood on the facade, the roof is finished in aluminum. A visitor center occupies the center of the building and overlooks the winery and vineyards, providing a serene space for wine tasting.

The design is a unique demonstration of the robustness of the principles of Calatrava's poetics, which can be adapted to a wide range of circumstances. At the same time it also shows how deeply his process is rooted in the region, respectful to a setting that owes its identity not only to its natural environment but also to its culture as a place of cultivation. The intricate geometry of the structure creates a strong profile but does not mimic the surrounding topography, with the snow-capped Pyrenees in the distance. It rides like a wave among their gently rolling forms rather than bearing down on them. Ysios recalls the remarkable sinusoidal line of the roof of Gaudí's so-called Small Schools adjacent to the Sagrada Familia. The ruled surface wave combines concave and convex surfaces as it evolves along the longitudinal axis. To give the impression of buoyancy, Calatrava located the base of the building within a reflective pool of water so that it seems to be in a state of suspended animation.

Opposite: Entrance
to visitor center.
Overleaf: Undulating
roof with Pyrenees in
background

This page: Interior view.
Opposite: Detail view
of roof

In 1998 Calatrava was asked to design two more bridges intended to mark the renewal of their surrounding areas: the James Joyce Bridge, Dublin, Ireland, and the Puente de la Mujer for Puerto Madero, the old harbor of Buenos Aires, Argentina. A single inclining pylon was proposed for both. For the Dublin bridge the idea of a bending bow scheme added an aspect of suspense and tension.

For the Buenos Aires bridge, Calatrava used a single inclined pylon 39 meters high, from which a rotating deck 102 meters long is suspended by cables and set between a pair of fixed bridges. The rotating section can turn 90 degrees to allow free passage of water traffic. The weight of the mechanical tower balances the weight of the pylon. The total bridge length is 160 meters. The material for the structure is reinforced concrete and steel, and for the pavement natural stone and ceramic. At night special lighting emphasizes the urban civic character of the area, which was redeveloped by La Corporación Antiguo Puerto Madero into a commercial, residential, and tourist district. In addition to its symbolic role, the bridge was expected to improve pedestrian routes inadequately connected to the urban fabric, as well as to the nearby axis created by the town hall, the Plaza de Mayo, and the Plaza Rosada. The footbridge for a dock still used for water traffic enhances pedestrian circulation and connects the plazas on either side of the embankment.

This page: View of single pylon. Opposite: View of bridge in operation. Overleaf: Bridge with surrounding urban context

The Turning Torso Apartment Tower, Malmö, Sweden, was designed in 1999 for the 2001 European Housing Expo, for a prominent urban site at the city's west harbor. The building signaled a new direction in the professional practice of Calatrava, as well as a new exploration into his poetics of movement. The scheme is derived from analogy to the human body as discussed in chapter 3, but it also emerged out of Calatrava's sculptural investigations. The project was intended as a landmark visible from a distance, giving a stronger identity to the area and defining the intersection of two main roads. The spiraling tower of the apartment building is composed of nine "town house" box units, each containing five floors. The units communicate through a nucleus of internal elevators and stairs.

Each town house unit totals approximately 2,200 square meters, with each floor accommodating one to five dwelling units around the vertical nucleus, where the "wet" spaces (kitchen, bathrooms, and closets) are allocated. Observation decks are provided in the spaces between units, while space in the spine unit may be used either for a premium residence or as a common area for tenants, meeting rooms, gyms, or technical space. Laundry, storage, and service areas are provided in the two subbasement floors. A corridor located at first-floor level connects the tower to a secondary building, which will feature shops at ground level and parking on the three upper levels. A covered arcade in front of the shops provides a pleasant zone for pedestrians. In addition to the interesting morphological aspects of the tower's configuration, the project explores a novel and intriguing collective housing type, which is developed further in the context of Manhattan.

View of model

Calatrava's project for the new Christ the Light Cathedral was selected through an invitational competition in 2000. The Cathedral of St. Francis de Sales, serving the Roman Catholic Diocese of Oakland, California, was severely damaged by the earthquake of 1989. The diocese decided to build a new cathedral with the specific goals of "creating an accessible, hospitable, culturally diverse gathering place, where the liturgy might flourish." The cathedral comprises 3,065 square meters and rises to a height of 30.5 meters, and seats 1,800 worshippers. It is conceived as a hospitable gathering place for both ritual and discussion, with a sanctuary core generating a concentric distribution of the assembly to facilitate visibility and participation. An ambulatory foyer surrounds the assembly and opens to a peripheral corridor accessible to the adjacent gardens. The main nave is treated as a shell, with a roof-wall system that defines the interior and exterior spaces. On the north-south axis a series of parallel walls carved in the form of an open arc defines the main space structurally and spatially. On the east-west axis two twin arches hold and bisect the walls, leaving a gap between for a skylight. Light plays an important role in its interplay with the structural elements, particularly as it flashes down through the triangular curved skylight to the nave. An external louver system allows for the control of natural light.

Recalling the roof motif of the Church of the Year 2000, Calatrava proposed a moving structure whereby two wings are transformed by analogy into two hands that almost touch and point upward. Movable elements allow the hands to be brought together in a gesture of prayer or opened to the sky. At first glance this is an extremely novel cathedral building, but upon closer inspection the organization of spaces, the configuration of the volumes, and the articulation of the structure are clearly drawn from the long tradition of ecclesiastical architecture and medieval buildings. In fact, Calatrava always included such examples in his notebooks. He revisited the moving roof device once more in the project for the Atlanta Symphony Orchestra Concert Hall in 2002. However, its use in the cathedral was particularly appropriate, suggesting in an accessible way an image of devotion.

This page: View of interior. Opposite: Model of building in urban context

Very different from the medieval world of forms inspiring the Christ the Light Cathedral is the spirit of the Master Plan for the 2004 Olympic and Paralympic Games, to be held in Athens. Despite the fact that the area in Calatrava's proposal is inhabited by structures reflecting the repertory of Calatrava's motifs and types, the overall composition has a strong neoclassical character.

The host city and the organizing committee of the 2004 Olympic and Paralympic Games resolved to improve and harmonize the existing Athens Olympic Sports Complex, its surrounding area, and its access routes. Calatrava—who was commissioned in 2001 to design a number of structures for the games, including a pedestrian bridge, a metro and railway station, and a sports complex—proposed a rigorous spatial reorganization of the site to serve athletes, the public, and the news media, as well as a permanent center for athletic and cultural events with an upgraded transportation system within an ecologically sustainable, parklike setting replete with olive trees and cypresses. Calatrava also conceived a new roof for the Olympic Stadium, a complete refurbishing of the Velodrome, various entrance plazas and entrance canopies for the complex, and a central Plaza of the Nations with tree-lined boulevards and a sculptural Nations Wall. The complex has a graceful, neoclassical character that recalls Athens before it became a crowded megalopolis.

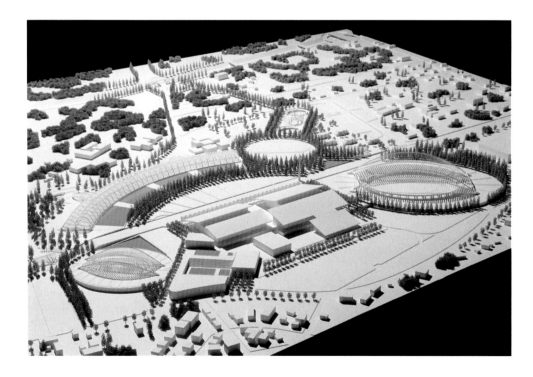

This page: Model of master plan. Opposite: Detail view of shaded promenade

View of shaded promenade

Velodrome

This page and opposite:
Views of stadium's new
suspended roof.
Previous pages: View
of complex at dusk

This page: Nations Wall.
Opposite: Detail of
Nations Wall

Expansion Plan for the Museo dell'Opera del Duomo Florence, Italy

The expansion of the Museo dell'Opera del Duomo, Florence, Italy, contains artworks and artifacts from Florence's great cathedral, Santa Maria del Fiore. It is one of the most important collections of sculpture from the early Renaissance through the Mannerist period, including Michelangelo's last *Pietà,* Donatello's *Magdalene,* the Baptistery doors of Ghiberti, and architectural wooden models by Brunelleschi for the cathedral's cupola as well as historic models and objects from centuries of building at the cathedral. The museum's governing body, the Opera di Santa Maria del Fiore—the same institution that during the Renaissance commissioned Giotto's campanile and Brunelleschi's cupola—resolved to double the size of the institution, from 2,000 square meters to 4,000 square meters, using the space of the former Teatro degli Intrepidi. The commission was awarded to Calatrava through an invitational competition. Calatrava reinterpreted the theme of vaulted space within his own framework of structure, proposing a new top-lit exhibition gallery with display areas for the museum's masterpieces.

This page: Drawing by Calatrava. Opposite: View of interior

| **Light Rail Train Bridge** Jerusalem, Israel

The city of Jerusalem, Israel, intending to enhance its transportation services, decided to introduce a light rail train system to connect various parts of the city and its environs. One of the new system's most important sites is near the central bus station, where the state-run intercity transportation system, the local and regional transportation systems, and the light rail system meet at the junction of Jaffa Road, the road that in ancient times connected the Old City of Jerusalem with Jaffa on the Mediterranean Sea; the Tel Aviv Highway, establishing the connection between Jerusalem and the Ben Gurion Airport and, further on, to Tel Aviv; and Herzl Boulevard, which leads to the Yad Vashem Holocaust Museum, Hadassah Medical Center, and the area encompassing the Knesset and the Supreme Court. Calatrava was invited to design a Light Rail Train (LRT) Bridge for this complex location, which was considered from the outset not only an infrastructure project but also a landmark structure that would function as a modern gateway to the city while maintaining continuity with the past.

Although its location is extremely significant, the site lacked distinction and was spatially amorphous. Thus in addition to a master plan for the site several alternative bridge schemes—an arch bridge and cable-stayed bridge, each with inclined, straight, or curved pylons—were proposed to ameliorate the site's immediate conditions. All of these schemes sought to enhance the pedestrian experience by offering a panoramic view of the landscape from the deck of the bridge. Calatrava also considered the impact of the structure on the existing urban context and on the future development of the area. The idea of a cable bridge, being the least intrusive, dominated the proposal process and was ultimately adopted with an inclined pylon and a bridge deck with a curved alignment. The pylon consists of a triangular steel box with its section diminishing toward the top; it inclines sideways as well as backward, toward the city and is visible from Herzl Boulevard, Jaffa Road, and the Tel Aviv Highway. The cables are arranged in a reverted alignment, generating a parabolic shape that appears to evolve three-dimensionally.

Indeed, most of these ideas were already researched and developed in Calatrava's studio for future use within his poetics of movement. Yet in Jerusalem the pylon rising like a ladder of light, the flame-shaped parabolic surface of the cable-sweep, and the progressive ascent of the deck—with their durable and delicate geometry —all appear as if they were conceived expressly for this landmark gateway.

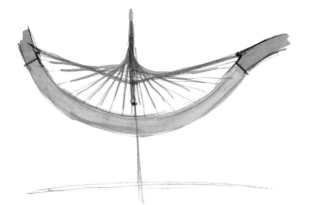

This page: Preliminary sketch by Calatrava. Opposite: Bridge as landmark for the city

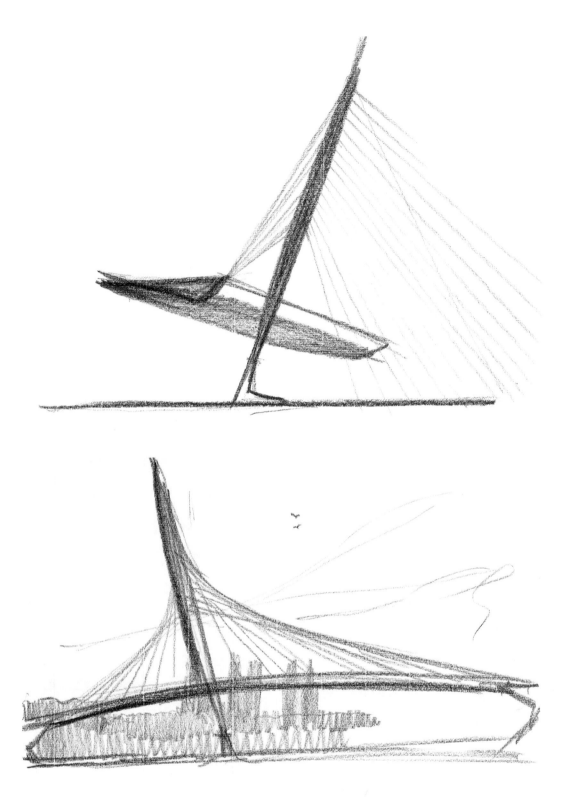

Preliminary sketches
by Calatrava

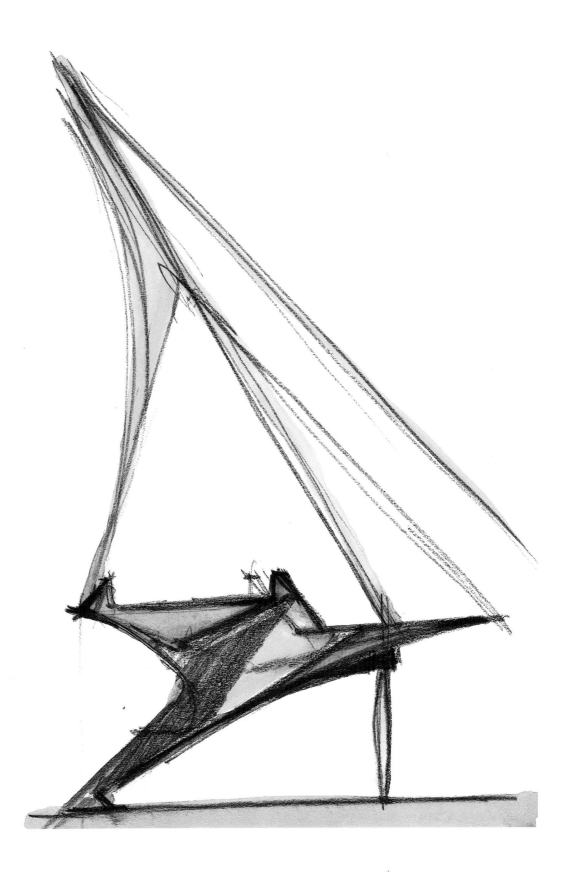

Views of bridge
approached from
either end

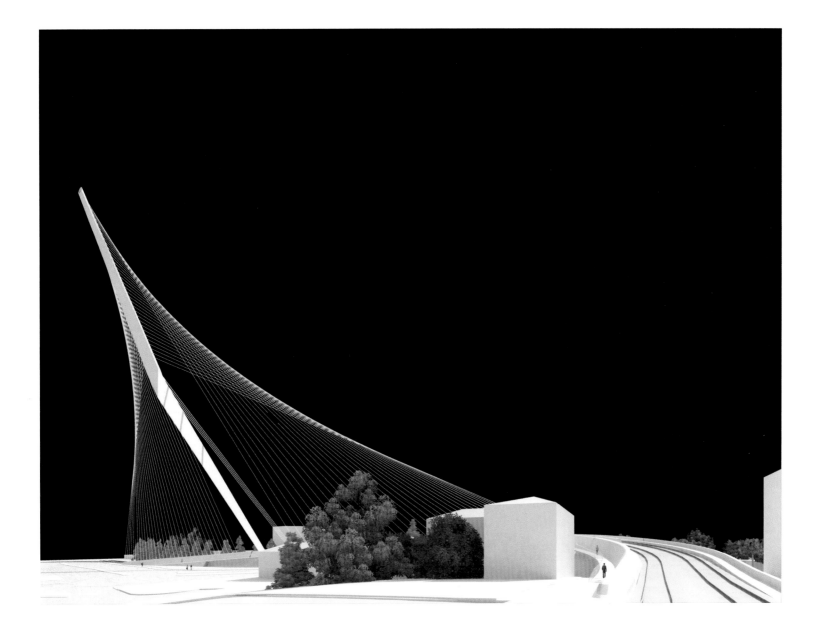

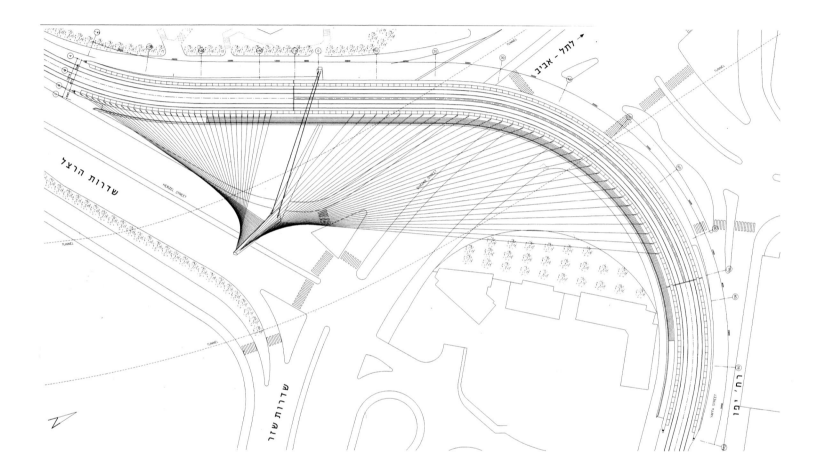

לתל - אביב →

שדרות הרצל

HERZEL STREET

GRAND STREET

אלנבי רחוב

HAIFA STREET

TUNNEL

TUNNEL

TUNNEL

נ, רחוב

This page: Plan.
Opposite: Elevations

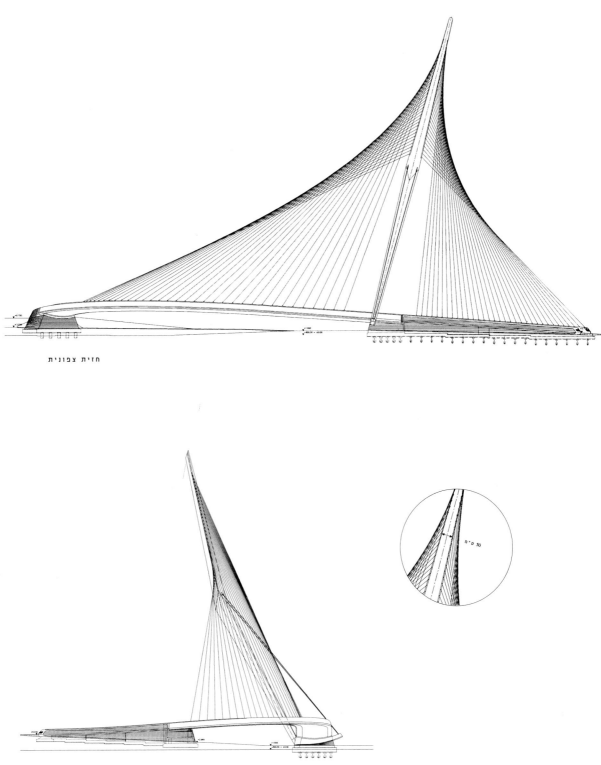

חזית צפונית

חזית מזרחית

50 ס"מ

Chapter 7 | Forms of the Body and the Spirit

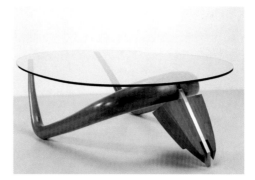
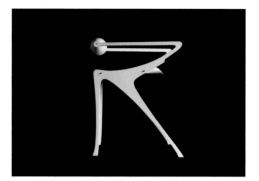

Despite the characteristic large scale of his projects, Calatrava engaged in designing furniture from the very beginning of his professional career. This was the result of his "total design" approach that in most of his projects entailed a complete responsibility for the product without distinctions of scale. As we have already seen, Calatrava always paid special attention to "infrastructure furniture," such as the details of his bridges, including railings, steps, and lighting fixtures. In the Tabourettli Theater, discussed in chapter 2, the stairs, shutters, coatracks, and ceiling features were specified to a scale of detail one usually sees in furniture design; he also designed actual furniture for the project as well, including the chairs and the counter of the cloakroom. Calatrava's complex multifunctional roof elements, beams, and light fixtures for the

Bärenmatte Community Center, also discussed in chapter 2, required similar attention to detail. The most important characteristic of the furniture, however, is not scale or detail but its intimate relationship to the human body. As Mario Praz noted in his celebrated *Illustrated History of Furnishing*, furniture is not only a "mold of the human body," waiting to receive, but also a "human counterpart," a "mold of the spirit": "The anthropomorphic and theriomorphic forms so frequent in furniture [indicate] how furniture shares in man's life."[1]

As a fascinating footnote, Edgar Allan Poe implies in his essay "Philosophy of Furniture" that the use of analogy in furniture design has more to do with human aspirations, desires, and delusions than problem solving.[2] Calatrava's furniture extensively uses analogies and formal

motifs that are deeply rooted in Western cultural tradition going as far back as the Greeks. As in Hellenistic and Roman furniture, Calatrava uses animal or human figures as points of generation. The human body appears by itself in various positions of rest or action or in combinations of these, as in the interlocked, ecstatic lovers made into a base for a table. The positions are choreographic, erotic, mythical, and oneiric. Surrealism has a strong presence here. It is widely acknowledged that classical dream constructs such as sphinxes, griffins, dolphins, swans, and lions—which one can discern in Calatrava's furniture—greatly inspired the Surrealists. The Surrealist fusion, melting, and transformation of one figure into another can also be seen in Calatrava's image navigation from, say, leaf to fish bone before reaching its final permutation as a

This page: Table with horn-shaped base (left); armchair (right). Opposite: Stepped-platform sofa

support for a table, and through this "migration" of forms Calatrava produces unprecedented configurations. An even more uncommon source of analogy is the horns of a bull. Horn-shaped components have often been used for utensil and furniture forms, but not to the degree of Calatrava's table support. The object has ritualistic, heroic nobility and produces an effect somewhere between Buñuel and Oldenburg, between the reverie of a dream and shock of coming awake.

The classical antecedents of Calatrava's furniture include the Directoire and Premier Empire styles, particularly in the X-shaped "interlocked lovers" of the table base, which recall Directoire tabouret legs and folding chairs. Equally reminiscent of the Directoire style, with echoes of the Greek klismos, is the elegant arm-chair. Even the seemingly unprecedented radical configuration of the stepped-platform sofa may be linked with the typical Directoire single headboard, whose ascending wave curve Calatrava translates into usable flat surfaces.

During the 1980s Calatrava produced a series of thirty-two tables, their number being derived from Bach's thirty-two *Goldberg Variations*. Superficially, any parallels between the *Goldberg Variations*, with its methodical divisions, repetitions, and intricate numerological structures, and the Calatrava tables would seem unlikely. Equally unlikely appears to be any association between the freewheeling forms of any of his furniture and a rigorous, rule-based generative system. Yet, if we try to suspend for the moment any analogical associations with objects, real or mythological, and we look at the formal-spatial characteristics of each piece of furniture, it becomes apparent that they are controlled by an order: distinctive delineations, successions, modulations, cadences, elisions, and other devices that are not so alien from the musical time-and-tone patterning mechanisms used by Bach.

As in a melodic development and variations, the profiles of the thirty-two tables rise, swell, stretch, bend, surge, turn, attach, clasp, return, weaken, contract, and end in a cadence. These tables—and by extension the rest of the furniture designed by Calatrava—tend to be organized across a range of ideas very similar to those that generated the folding structures, bridges, and sculptures. The presence of the body and spirit in these phases of space go much deeper than mere anthropomorphic depictions.

Studies for a table base,
by Calatrava

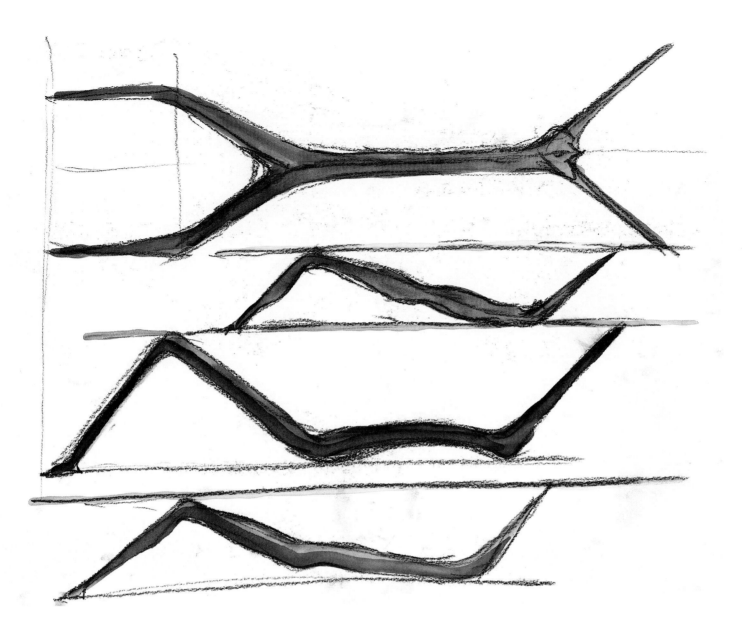

Drawings of horn-
shaped components,
by Calatrava

Table

Table

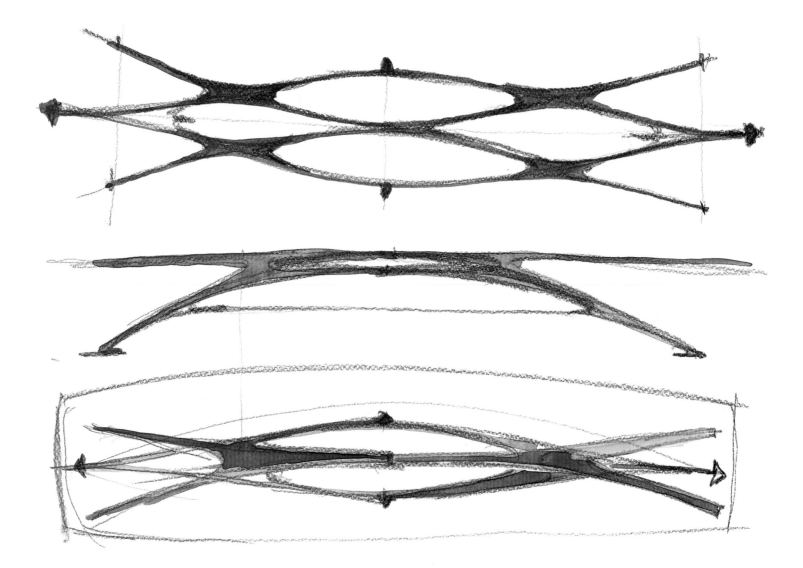

Studies for a table,
by Calatrava

Table

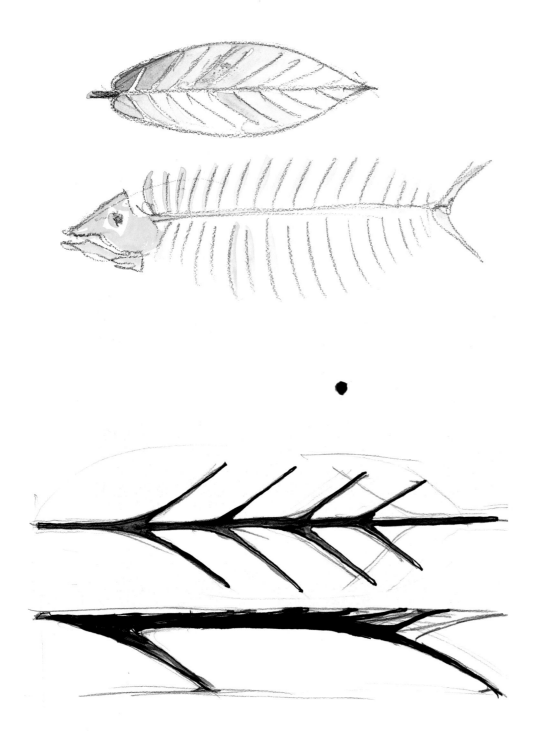

This page: Studies for
a table, by Calatrava.
Opposite: Table

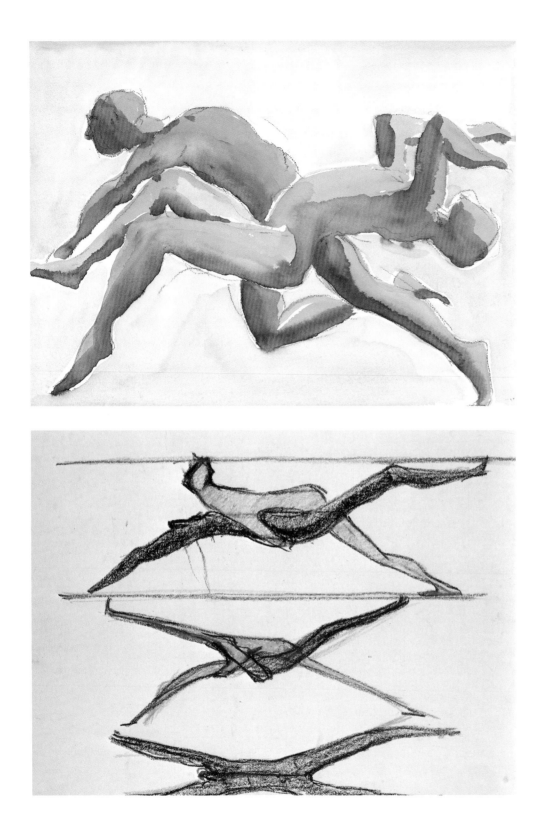

This page: Studies of human figures for a table base, by Calatrava. Opposite: *Interlocked Lovers* table

Epilogue | White Time

Like most of the basic qualities that characterize Calatrava's work, the rare ability of his projects to enhance their surrounding environment and to infuse it with a sense of anticipation and joy, while at the same time maintaining a strong visual profile, has its roots in the period of his self-education in Valencia. As noted in chapter 1, in the early 1970s Calatrava, with a small number of fellow students, took advantage of the freedom offered by the crisis of the formal university system to study Mediterranean vernacular structures. He looked at these structures as a source of experience and "a song of hope for the new architecture," particularly in terms of their unique success in relating to their physical and historical milieu. Calatrava wrote the following poem during the documentation of these buildings:

With a sea
With the rocks
With the foam
And the seagulls
Of an encounter

Of an encounter with time passed,
With time present,
With time without end,
With a white time.

Among these structures occupying this poetic "white time" the most impressive was a mill that for Calatrava suggested a general approach toward building and environment rather than a particular region or epoch. Calatrava described the structure as a "short and direct answer through rational construction methods to functional demands." The mill was "composed of a series of volumes attached to one another forming a total body of multiple facets, the singular poetics of the cluster," appearing in the landscape as "a break, a point of attention, a pause." It is precisely these qualities that Calatrava imported from the land of "white time," the Mediterranean of his youth, to each of the challenging sites where he would be involved in his practice as an architect, an engineer, and a sculptor around the globe, including, during the last decade, the United States.

* * *

The redesign of the Cathedral of St. John the Divine was Calatrava's first New York City project. It was followed in 1995 by the Southpoint

80 South Street Tower, New York, photomontages of building with surrounding urban context (opposite and page 377) and view of model (page 378)

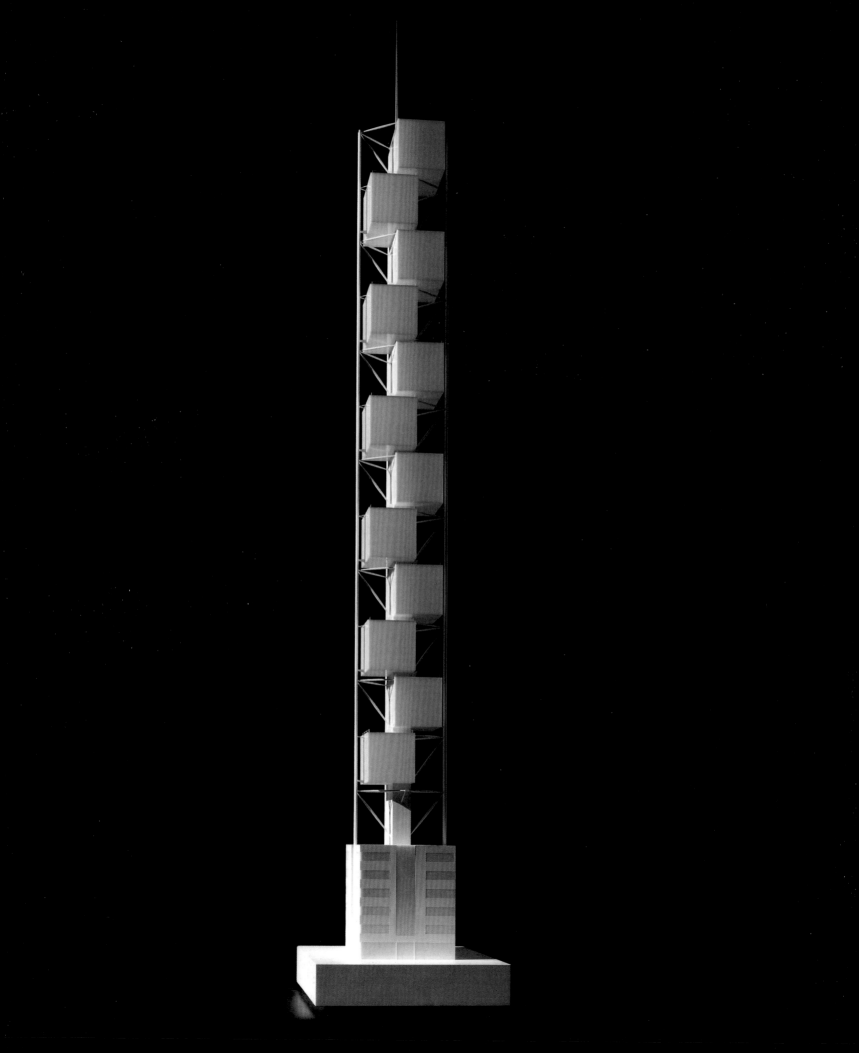

Pavilion, a terminal for the ferry between Manhattan and Roosevelt Island. The project was part of a comprehensive redevelopment plan for the southern end of Roosevelt Island, on the East River between Manhattan and Queens. The pavilion is located on the west edge of a park adjacent to Louis Kahn's memorial for Franklin Delano Roosevelt and faces the United Nations across the water. Calatrava proposed a visitor center with a restaurant and facilities for exhibitions and banquets, and he conceived a glass-roofed shell circular in plan and resting on a concrete base clad in the same stone used for the surrounding paved terraces. The pavilion is protected by a movable structure composed of thin aluminium fins that open and close as a folding brise-soleil. The resulting contrast with the surrounding context is not offensive or aggressive. Inspired by Mediterranean precedents, Cala-

trava thrust forward the movable structure so that it would appear as a "break" or "pause" among the existing built fabric. The idea was reworked for two other American projects—the Christ the Light Cathedral in Oakland and the shrine on Cathedral Square in Los Angeles—and finally materialized, as we have seen, in the Milwaukee Art Museum.

Similarly, 80 South Street Tower in lower Manhattan, designed by Calatrava in 2000, stands apart from the rest of the towers of New York while simultaneously enhancing their identity. The tower stands at the East River, at South and Fletcher streets, near the South Street Seaport and the Brooklyn Bridge. The building's program includes, in addition to the residential facilities, a museum and space for cultural uses. Its total height above ground level is 1,111 feet with occupiable space rising

855 feet. Residences are located within a series of twelve glazed 48-foot-square cubes, each of which is four stories high and is intended to house one or two families. The cubes are cantilevered in ladderlike steps up the structure's slim core. Sixty-three of the tower's seventy-four floors are inhabited, and an additional twelve terrace levels brings the total square footage to 175,000. The principal materials are concrete and steel.*

The modular scheme of the tower owes much to previous sculptural experiments involving cumulative forms of cubes. In particular, the configuration strongly resembles the Turning Torso sculpture with cubic units attached to a spinal cordlike support and twisted around an axis like vertebrae. Yet, as was mentioned in chapter 5, the sculptural composition trial was autonomous. The potentials of the configuration

* Developer: F.J. Sciame Construction Co., Inc.; Sciame Development, Inc. Design Team: Christian Brändle (project manager); Hanspeter Müller, Dario Viola, Lorenzo Gottardi, Matthias Hochuli, Sandro de Roma, Bruno Stoekenius (architects); Ricardo Gómez Frías (Renderings), Pascal Guinard, Luigi Razzano (project structural engineer)

to be applied for designing a residential building became evident later. Another precedent for 80 South Street Tower is the Turning Torso Tower in Malmö.

Apart from the visual, spatial-compositional aspects of the tower and its possible implied symbolic meanings, the architectural significance of 80 South Street Tower lies in the new kind of residential type it introduces to architecture and specifically to New York. Reminiscent of Moshe Safdie's Habitat '67 complex in Montreal, but at a more daring scale, Calatrava's vertical scheme offers an innovative residential structure that maximizes lifestyle choices by combining characteristics of the high-rise (distant views and privacy) with those of the town house ones (variety of multilevel internal spaces and outdoor courts). Obviously the construction costs for such a solution are not low. However,

the benefits are tremendous: the new residential type of building offers a genuine alternative to suburbia, overcoming the limitations of traditional apartments or row houses.

Even more defiant in the context of the architecture of Manhattan, while at the same time contributing enormously to it, was Calatrava's scheme for the World Trade Center Transportation Hub. The project not only assisted in solving practical problems posed by the destruction of this vital transportation exchange center, but it also has aided in the process of healing the severe psychological trauma produced by the events of September 11, 2001. The complex is primarily a permanent transportation focal point for Lower Manhattan serving riders of the Port Authority Trans-Hudson (PATH) commuter trains and the New York City subway trains (1/9 and N/R lines), and offering a potential rail link to the air-

port. In addition, according to the official brief, it is expected to provide seamless indoor pedestrian access to the World Financial Center, adjacent buildings, and the proposed new Fulton Street Transit Center. Further on, it is expected to act as a catalyst to revive urban activities around the clock in the area. The Calatrava scheme added a cultural component to this program. The specific location is immediately to the east of the footprint of the Twin Towers. The site is bounded by the Ground Zero Memorial on the west and Church Street on the east, Fulton Street on the north and Dey Street on the south.

Given the tremendous technical complexity of the project, the client, the Port Authority of New York and New Jersey, invited a small number of qualified specialized firms to participate in the competition, which was won by Calatrava. Collaborating with Calatrava was the Downtown

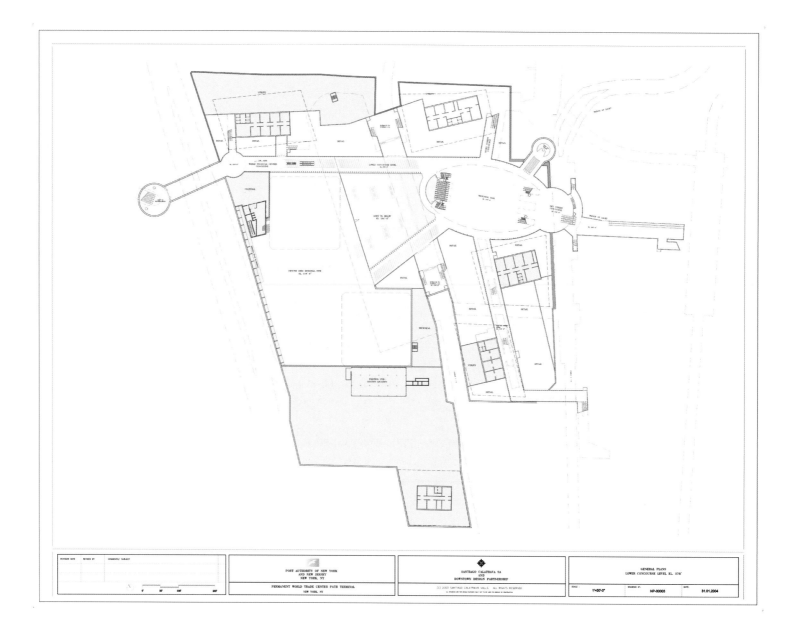

Design Partnership, a joint venture of DMJM + Harris and STV Group. The estimated cost was $2 billion.

The project is situated within a landscaped plaza (approximately 410 by 225 feet) that has been conceived through the re-creation of Fulton and Dey streets west of Church Street. The scheme is divided into two major components: the structure visible at street level and an underground complex. The structure above grade is designed as a freestanding object made out of glass and steel whose construction implies a modification of Daniel Libeskind's initial plan, which placed the entrance to the station adjacent to a tower. With this change, the volume of the hub above ground and the space surrounding it offers yet another break, or pause, amid the dense buildings planned for the site. Even more, treating the volume of the station visible at street level as an autonomous object provided the hub

with an urban identity and architectural expression. In addition, according to the brief, this treatment of the site helped to create a link in a procession of green spaces, which will extend down Park Row from City Hall Park to the churchyard of St. Paul's Chapel, then through the World Trade Center Transportation Hub plaza to the garden of the memorial. Conforming to Libeskind's master plan for the site the building is angled to sit along the southern edge of the "Wedge of Light" plaza that is part of his master plan.

The design of the part of the building visible at street level has very little to do with stations previously designed by Calatrava. But it does draw from previous experiments that addressed the problem of relating an underground complex with an urban setting above it, as in the Alcoy Community Hall, the Emergency Services Center in St. Gallen, and the unbuilt Southpoint Pavilion

World Trade Center Transportation Hub, New York, computer rendering (this page) and main concourse level (opposite)

World Trade Center
Transportation Hub,
New York, computer
rendering of interior

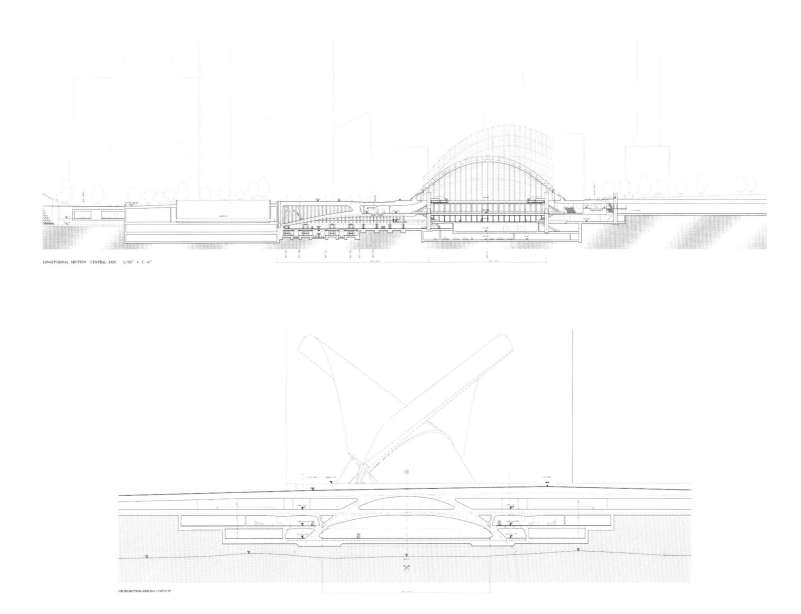

LONGITUDINAL SECTION CENTRAL AXIS 1/32" = 1'-0"

CROSS SECTION AXIS D14 1/16"=1'-0"

World Trade Center
Transportation Hub,
New York, sections

in New York. The arched oval of glass and steel is approximately 375 feet long, spans 110 feet at its widest point, and is 75 feet high at its apex. The steel ribs that support this structure extend upward into a pair of canopies that resemble outspread wings and rise to a maximum height of 150 feet. On the main concourse—approximately 40 feet below street level and 120 feet below the apex of the glass roof—visitors will be able to look up at a column-free, clear span.

Calatrava has stated that the configuration of this structure was inspired by the image of a bird released from a child's hand. This is not the first time that Calatrava refers to such an image in relation to a moving, winglike structure. On the other hand, given the context of the September 11 tragedy, the bird figure becomes a unique symbol most appropriate for the site and the occasion. Indeed, this is one of the reasons the project was received with such overwhelming enthusiasm by the public.

Aside from the idea of the bird configuration, the public was also impressed by the emphasis Calatrava put on the presence of light and the way it penetrates the structure in his public presentation and in all public discussions. Characteristically, the brief includes among the principal materials of construction—glass, steel, concrete, and stone—light as one of the materials. The covering, referred above, allows daylight to flood into the underground space of the World Trade Center Transportation Hub, penetrating through all levels by means of glass-block floors to the train platform, approximately 70 feet below the street. And, as in Alcoy, at night the direction of light is reversed so that the structure is illuminated from the space underground like a lantern.

Certainly the enthusiastic reception of the theme of light relates to its symbolic role as a powerful vitalizing force. In a very schematic way this celebration of light, rather than the brute force of height, appeared as the most proper—and the most universal—representation of optimism. Reinforcing this message is the presence of explicit physical movement: the structure's "wings" unfold on fine days in spring and summer, expressing further the sense of chthonic darkness mitigated by exposure to the greater world.

In this sense Calatrava opted for an iconological repertory that describes timelessness and a cyclical, year-round process to emphasize the triumph of regeneration and revitalization rather

Opposite and following pages: Drawings by Calatrava

than the memory of a single point in time that represents only catastrophe. Only on September 11 each year will the roof part to its maximum opening of 45 feet, bringing into the building a slice of sky and its light at an angle commemorating the tragic events of that day in 2001.

Access to the building at street level is provided by four entrances: an east pair (on the Church Street side) and a west pair (near Greenwich Street). Each pair of entrances opens onto an escalator and stair landing. Elevators, which are cylindrical, are also provided at each entrance. From the entrance, visitors will descend approximately 22 feet to the upper concourse level, where the ovoid interior space opens to its full dimensions (approximately 415 by 190 feet). From here, visitors have access to subway lines and the Fulton Street Transit Center. Visitors descend another 20 feet to the main concourse level through escalators, elevators, and stairs to gain access to connections to neighboring buildings (including the World Financial Center), as well as potential pedestrian connections to the World Trade Center memorial site and a proposed airport rail link. Descending another 14 feet, visitors reach the mezzanine level, with ticketing and other services for the PATH trains. Though the PATH platform level is approximately 70 feet below street level, natural light still reaches down to it by way of glass-block floors. In a reversal of the conventional concept of how light works in a structure, Calatrava has said that the building is supported by "columns of light"—"metaphysical," symbolic light, but also physical light.

Calatrava's scheme for the World Trade Center Transportation Hub complex appears to offer back to New York not only a piece of what the September 11 tragedy had taken away, but also something that New York has been deprived of due to a long period of uncertainty, lack of vision, and a moribund civic spirit: the making of large-scale, public urban and infrastructure projects serving and celebrating the community in the manner of the Brooklyn Bridge, Central Park, Pennsylvania Station, and Grand Central Terminal. One must add that this conspicuous absence of civic-minded projects is not only typical of the recent history of New York City. It is a global condition typical of our time, making Calatrava's scheme, and his entire oeuvre, a gift to the city of New York as well as to the world.

Drawings by Calatrava

Notes, Bibliography, Biography

Prologue

1. David W. Dunlap, "A PATH Station That Honors 9/11, and Opens Wide, Too," *New York Times*, 23 January 2004, B1.

2. Henri Bergson, *The Creative Mind*, trans. Mabelle L. Andison (New York: Philosophical Library, 1946); Alexander Tzonis, *Santiago Calatrava, The Poetics of Movement* (New York: Universe Publishing, 1999).

Chapter 1

1. Liane Lefaivre, *Santiago Calatrava: Wie ein Vogel / Like a Bird* (Geneva and Milan: Skira, 2003).

2. Santiago Calatrava Archive.

3. Le Corbusier, *New World of Space* (New York: Reynal & Hitchcock, 1948).

4. Santiago Calatrava, "Zur Faltbarkeit von Fachwerken" (*On the Foldability of Space Frames*, Ph.D. dissertation, 1981), as reproduced in Alexander Tzonis, *Santiago Calatrava's Creative Process I: Fundamentals* (Basel, Switzerland: Birkhäuser Verlag, 2001). Calatrava's thesis abstract summarized the research as follows: "The work describes the geometrical principles applying to the construction of foldable, load-bearing frames. The objective of this work is to formulate geometrical relationships and systematically investigate those relationships and their application to structures composed of bars and nodal connections (frames) in order to obtain foldable structures. Particular emphasis is placed on the investigation of "Basic Modular Elements" for the formation of foldable structures. The arrangement of these elements in both planar and spatial grids permits the formation of frames which, in addition to their primary function as load-bearing structures, are designed to be foldable." William Zuk, *Kinetic Architecture* (New York: Van Nostrand Reinhold, 1970). R.H. MacNeal, J.M. Hedgepeth, and H.U. Schuerch, "Heliogyro Solar Sailer Summary Report" (Washington, D.C.: NASA contractor report, 1969); H.U. Schuerch and J.M. Hedgepeth, "Large Low-Frequency Orbiting Radio Telescope" (Washington, D.C.: NASA contractor report, 1968); R.F. Crawford, J.M. Hedgepeth, and P.R. Preiswerk, "Spoked Wheels to Deploy Large Surfaces in Space—Weight Estimates for Scolar Arrays" (Washington, D.C.: NASA contractor report, 1975); J. Onoda, N. Watanabe, K. Ichida, Y. Hashimoto, A. Nakada, and H. Saito, "Two-Dimensional Deployable 'SHDF' Truss," report no. 633 (Tokyo: The Institute of Space and Astronautical Science, 1988); "AAFE Large Deployable Antenna Development Program" (Washington, D.C.: NASA contractor report, 1977); J.M. Hedgepeth and L.R. Adama, "Design Concepts for Large Reflector Antenna Structures" (Washington, D.C.: NASA contractor report, 1983).

5. Alexander Tzonis, "Huts, Ships and Bottleracks: Design by Analogy for Architects and/or Machines," in N. Cross, et al., eds., *Research in Design Thinking* (Delft, Netherlands: Delft University of Technology, 1992).

Drawing by Calatrava

Chapter 2

1. Gottfried Semper, "Style: The Textile Art," in *The Four Elements of Architecture and Other Writings*, trans. Harry Francis Mallgrave and Wolfgang Herrmann (Cambridge and New York: Cambridge University Press, 1989), 254ff.

Chapter 3

1. Examples of a complete notebook by Calatrava were published and introduced in Alexander Tzonis and Liane Lefaivre, *Santiago Calatrava's Creative Process II: Sketchbooks* (Basel, Switzerland: Birkhäuser Verlag, 2001).

2. I.B. Hart, *The Mechanical Investigations of Leonardo da Vinci* (Berkeley, Calif.: University of California Press, 1963).

3. Keith J. Holyoak and Paul Thagard, *Mental Leaps* (Cambridge: MIT Press, 1995); Robert J. Sternberg and Janet E. Davidson, *The Nature of Insight* (Cambridge: MIT Press, 1995); P. Langley, H.A. Simon, G.L. Bradshaw, and J.M. Zytkow, *Scientific Discovery: Computational Explorations of the Creative Processes* (Cambridge: MIT Press, 1987); J. Hadamard, *The Psychology of Invention in the Mathematical Field* (New York: Dover Publications, 1954); P. Langley, H.A. Simon, G.L. Bradshaw, and J.M. Zytkow, *Scientific Discovery: Computational Explorations of the Creative Processes* (Cambridge: MIT Press, 1987).

4. Richard Lewontin, "The Evolution of Cognition," in Daniel N. Osherson and Edward E. Smith, eds., *An Invitation to Cognitive Science* (Cambridge: MIT Press, 1990).

5. Liane Lefaivre, *Leon Battista Alberti's Hypnerotomachia Poliphili* (Cambridge: MIT Press, 1997).

6. Liane Lefaivre, *Santiago Calatrava, Wie ein Vogel / Like a Bird* (Geneva and Milan: Skira, 2003); Sigmund Freud, "The Relation of the Poet to Daydreaming," in Philip Rieff, ed., *Delusion and Dream* (Boston: Beacon Press, 1956), 122–34. See also Sigmund Freud, *The Interpretation of Dreams*, in *Standard Edition of the Complete Works of Sigmund Freud*, trans. James Strachey (London: Hogarth Press, 1959). For a critical view of Freud's ideas on dreaming, see G. William Domhoff, "The Misinterpretation of Dreams," *American Scientist* (March–April 2000): 175–78, reviewing a new translation of Sigmund Freud's *Interpretation of Dreams* by Ritchie Robertson (Oxford: Oxford University Press, 1999).

7. Lewis Mumford, "Surrealism and Civilization," *The New Yorker* (19 December 1936): 79. For the liberating function of Surrealism, see André Breton, *Manifestoes of Surrealism*, trans. Richard Seaver and Helen R. Lane (Ann Arbor, Mich.: University of Michigan Press, 1972). Breton mentions Johan Huizinga's "*homo ludens*" in his 1954 essay "L'un dans l'autre."

8. Giovanni Paolo Lomazzo, *Trattato dell'arte de la pittura* (Milan: Apresso Paolo Gottardo Pontion, 1584).

9. Gotthold Ephraim Lessing, *Laocoon, an Essay upon the Limits of Painting and Poetry* (New York: Dutton, 1959). First published as *Laokoon: oder Über die Grenzen der Malerei und Poesie,* 1766.

Chapter 5

1. M. Levin, *Santiago Calatrava Artworks* (Basel, Switzerland: Birkhäuser Verlag, 2003).

2. Quoted by Donald Judd in *Perspecta* 11 (March–May 1968), which is reprinted in Donald Judd, *Complete Writings, 1959–1975* (New York: New York University Press, 1975).

3. Naum Gabo, "Constructivism," *Horizon* (July 1944): 60.

4. Baruch Spinoza, "On the Origins and Nature of Emotions," in Part III of *The Ethics.* See also Alexander Tzonis, introduction to *Santiago Calatrava, Structures and Movement*, by R. Hashimshoni (Haifa, Israel: Technion Institute of Technology, 1997).

5. Giulio Carlo Argan and others have argued that the "*non finito*" in Michelangelo's work was probably part of his general preoccupation with movement, the subject of a treatise he planned to write, as we know from Asciano Condivi, *Vita di Michelangelo Buonarroti,* 1553, reissued as *The Life of Michelangelo* (Baton Rouge, La.: Louisiana State University Press, 1976), also cited in David Summers, *Michelangelo and the Language of Art* (Princeton, N.J.: Princeton University Press, 1981), 406. For extensive discussion of the "*non finito*" and Calatrava's work, see Alexander Tzonis and Liane Lefaivre, *Movement, Structure and the Work of Santiago Calatrava* (Basel, Switzerland: Birkhäuser Verlag, 1994).

Chapter 7

1. Mario Praz, *An Illustrated History of Furnishing, from the Renaissance to the 20th Century* (New York: George Braziller, 1964).

2. Edgar Allan Poe, *The Philosophy of Furniture*, first published in *Burton's Gentleman's Magazine* in 1840 and with modifications in *Broadway Journal* in 1845.

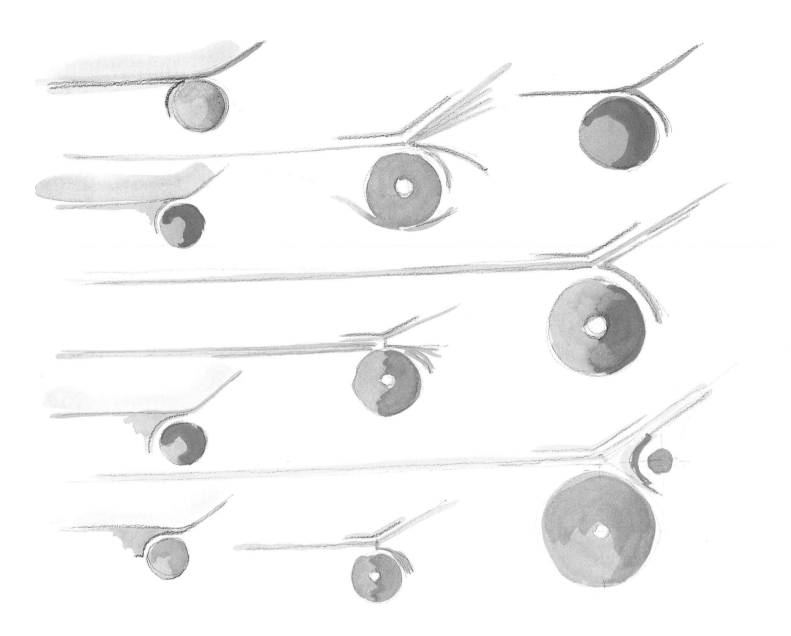

Bibliography | Monographs on the Work of Santiago Calatrava

Blaser, W. *Santiago Calatrava: Ingenieur Architektur/Engineering Architecture.* Basel, Switzerland: Birkhäuser Verlag, 1989.

Calatrava, S. *Santiago Calatrava—Conversations with Students*. C.L. Kausel and A. Pendleton-Jullian, eds. New York: Princeton Architectural Press, 2002.

Frampton, K., A.C. Webster, and A. Tischhauser. *Calatrava Bridges*. Zurich: Artemis Verlag, 1993.

Harbison, R. *Creatures from the Mind of the Engineer: The Architecture of Santiago Calatrava*. Zurich: Artemis Verlag, 1992.

Herrmanns, R. *Santiago Calatrava: Förverkligar det overkliga*. Stockholm: Bokförlag Läseleket, 2001.

Jodidio, P. *Oriente Station.* Lisbon: Centralivros Lda., 1998.

———. *Santiago Calatrava.* Köln: Benedikt Taschen, 1998.

Klein, B. *Santiago Calatrava: Bahnhof Stadelhofen, Zürich.* Berlin: Ernst Wasmuth Verlag, 1993.

Lefaivre, L., and A. Tzonis. *Santiago Calatrava's Creative Process II: Sketchbooks.* Basel, Switzerland: Birkhäuser Verlag, 2001.

Levin, M. *Calatrava: Drawings and Sculptures.* Weinfelden: Wolfau-Druck Rudolf Mühlemann, 2000.

———. *Santiago Calatrava Artworks*. Basel, Switzerland: Birkhäuser Verlag, 2003.

Pisani, M., E. Sicignano, and D. Mandolesi. *Santiago Calatrava: Progetti e Opere.* Rome: CDP, 1997.

Sharp, D., ed. *Santiago Calatrava.* London: Art/E&FN Spon, 1992.

Tischauser, A., and S. von Moos. *Public Buildings.* Basel, Switzerland: Birkhäuser Verlag, 1998.

Tzonis, A. *Santiago Calatrava: The Poetics of Movement.* New York: Universe Publishing, 1999.

———. *Santiago Calatrava's Creative Process I: Fundamentals.* Basel, Switzerland: Birkhäuser Verlag, 2001.

Tzonis, A., and L. Lefaivre. *Movement, Structure and the Work of Santiago Calatrava.* Basel, Switzerland: Birkhäuser Verlag, 1994.

Webster, A.C., and K. Frampton. *Santiago Calatrava.* Zurich: Schriftenreihe 15, Schule und Museum für Gestaltung, 1992.

Zardini, M. *Santiago Calatrava: Libro segreto.* Milan: Federico Motta Editore, 1995.

———. *Santiago Calatrava: Secret Sketchbook.* New York: Monacelli Press, 1996.

Drawings by Calatrava

Bibliography | Exhibition Publications, Special Issues of Periodicals, Project Monographs

Santiago Calatrava. Valencia, Spain: Generalitat Valenciana, 1986.

Santiago Calatrava. Zurich: Galerie Jamileh Weber, 1986.

"Santiago Calatrava 1983–1989." *El Croquis* 38, 1989.

"Santiago Calatrava 1990–1992." *El Croquis* 57, 1992.

"Santiago Calatrava 1983–1993." Valencia, Spain: La Lontja, 1993; reprinted as an editorial in *El Croquis*, 1993.

Santiago Calatrava Buildings and Bridges. Moscow: Europa Akademie, 1994.

Santiago Calatrava: The Dynamics of Equilibrium. Tokyo: Gallery MA, 1994.

Santiago Calatrava. Pamplona, Spain: Museo de Navarra, 1995.

Santiago Calatrava: Esculturas y Dibujos/Sculptures and Drawings. Valencia, Spain: IVAM Centre Julio González, Aldeasa-IVAM, 2001.

Blanco, M. *Santiago Calatrava.* Valencia, Spain: Generalitat Valenciana, 1999.

Campos, B. *Auditorio de Tenerife: Visiones/Visions.* Tenerife, Spain: Auditorio de Tenerife S.A., 2003.

Cullen, M.S., and M. Kieren. *Calatrava Berlin Five Projects/Fünf Projekte.* Basel, Switzerland: Birkhäuser Verlag, 1994.

Galiano, L.F. "Santiago Calatrava 1983–1996." *AV Monografías* 61, 1996.

Hashimshoni, R. *Santiago Calatrava: Structures and Movement.* Haifa, Israel: Technion, 1997.

Hauser, H. *Kontroverse Beitrage zu einem unstrittenen Bautypus*. Stuttgart: n.p., 1993.

Klein, B., K. Frampton, L. Schmutz, and P. Rice. "*Ein Bahnhof/Une gare.*" *Archithese* 2, 1990.

Le Roux, M., and M. Rivoire. *Calatrava: Escale Satolas.* Grenoble, France: Glenat, 1994.

Ledbetter, J.A. *Santiago Calatrava: Structures in Movement*. Hong Kong: South China Printing, 2001.

Lefaivre, L. *Santiago Calatrava: Wie ein Vogel/Like a Bird*. Geneva and Milan: Skira, 2003.

McQuaid, M. *Santiago Calatrava: Structure and Expression.* New York: Museum of Modern Art, 1992.

Molinari, L. *Santiago Calatrava*. Milan: Skira, 1998.

Nicolin, P. "Santiago Calatrava. Il folle vol/The Daring Flight." *Quaderni di Lotus* 7.

Polano, S. *Santiago Calatrava: Complete Works*. Milan: Electa, 1996.

Sharp, D. "Santiago Calatrava." *Architectural Monographs* 46, 1996.

Tischauser, A., and T. Kobler. *Santiago Calatrava: Dynamische Gleichgewichte Neue Projekte/Dynamic Equilibrium Recent Projects*. Zurich: Artemis Verlag, 1991.

Trame, U. *Opera Progretto: Santiago Calatrava Quadracci Pavilion, Milwaukee Art Museum*. Bologna: Editrice Compositori, 2001.

Webster, A.C., and K. Frampton. "Santiago Calatrava." Museum für Gestaltung, Zürich; Wolfau-Druck Rudolf Mühlemann, Weinfeld, 1992.

Biography	Santiago Calatrava

1951	Santiago Calatrava Valls born in the Benimamet district of Valencia, Spain
1968	School graduation in Valencia
1968–69	Attends Valencia School of Arts and Crafts
1969–74	Studies architecture at the Escuela Técnica Superior de Arquitectura de Valencia, qualifying as an architect followed by a postgraduate course in urbanism
1975–79	Studies civil engineering at the Swiss Federal Institute of Technology (ETH), Zurich
1979–81	Doctorate in Technical Science at ETH; Ph.D. dissertation: *On the Foldability of Space Frames*
	Assistant at the Institute for Building Statics and Construction and the Institute for Aerodynamics and Lightweight Construction at ETH
1981	Architectural and engineering practice established in Zurich
1982	Membership, International Association for Bridge & Structural Engineering, Zurich
1985	*9 Sculptures by Santiago Calatrava*, exhibition, Jamileh Weber Gallery, Zurich
1986	*Skulpturen und Brücken*, exhibition, Centro Cultural de la Caja de Ahorros, Valencia
1987	Member of BSA (Union of Swiss Architects)
	Auguste Perret UIA Prize (Union Internationale d'Architectes), Paris
	Member of the International Academy of Architecture, Sofia, Bulgaria
	Participation at the 17th Triennale in Milan
	Santiago Calatrava, exhibition, Museum of Architecture, Basel, Switzerland
1988	City of Barcelona Art Prize for the Bach de Roda Bridge, Barcelona
	Premio de la Asociación de la Prensa (Press Association Award), Valencia
	IABSE Prize, International Association of Bridge and Structural Engineering, Helsinki, Finland

FAD Prize, Fomento de las Artes y del Diseño, Spain

Fritz Schumacher Prize for Urbanism, Architecture and Engineering, Hamburg, Germany

Fazlur Rahman Khan International Fellowship for Architecture and Engineering

1989   Second architectural and engineering practice established in Paris

Honorary Member of BDA (Bund Deutscher Architekten)

Santiago Calatrava, traveling exhibition, New York, St. Louis, Chicago, Los Angeles, Toronto, Montreal

1990   Médaille d'Argent de la Recherche et de la Technique, Fondation Académie d'Architecture 1970, Paris

1991   European Glulam Award (Glued Laminated Timber Construction), Munich

Santiago Calatrava, exhibition, Suomen Rakennustaiteen Museum, Helsinki

City of Zurich Award for Good Building 1991, for Stadelhofen Railway Station, Zurich

Retrospective—Dynamic Equilibrium, exhibition, Museum of Design, Zurich

1992   CEOE Foundation, VI Dragados y Construcciones Prize for Alamillo Bridge, Spain

Honorary Member of Real Academia de Bellas Artes de San Carlos, Valencia

Member of the Europe Academy, Cologne, Germany

Retrospective, exhibition, Dutch Institute for Architecture, Rotterdam, The Netherlands

Gold Medal, Institute of Structural Engineers, London

Brunel Award, for Stadelhofen Railway Station, Zurich

Santiago Calatrava—Retrospective, exhibition, Royal Institute of British Architects, London

Retrospective, exhibition, Arkitektur Museet, Stockholm

1993   II Honor Prize, from the City of Pedreguer for Urban Architectonic Merit, Pedreguer, Spain

Santiago Calatrava—Bridges, exhibition, Deutsches Museum, Munich

Structure and Expression, exhibition, Museum of Modern Art, New York

Honorary Member of the Royal Institute of British Architects, London

Santiago Calatrava, exhibition, La Lontja Museum, Valencia

Santiago Calatrava, exhibition, Overbeck Society pavilion, Lübeck, Germany

Santiago Calatrava, exhibition, Architecture Centre, Gammel Dok, Copenhagen

Doctor Honoris Causa, Polytechnic University of Valencia

Medalla de Honor al Fomento de la Invención, Fundación García Cabrerizo, Madrid

City of Toronto Urban Design Award, for the BCE Place Gallery, Toronto

World Economic Forum Davos honours Santiago Calatrava as *Global Leader for Tomorrow*

1994   *Santiago Calatrava—Recent Projects*, exhibition, Bruton Street Gallery, London

Doctor Honoris Causa, University of Seville

Santiago Calatrava—Buildings and Bridges, exhibition, Museum of Applied and Folk Arts, Moscow

Creu de Sant Jordi, Generalitat de Catalunya, Barcelona

Doctor Honoris Causa of Letters in Environmental Studies, Heriot-Watt University, Edinburgh

Santiago Calatrava—The Dynamics of Equilibrium, exhibition, Gallery MA, Tokyo

Santiago Calatrava, exhibition, Arquería de los Nuevos Ministerios, Madrid

Santiago Calatrava, exhibition, Sala de Arte "La Recova," Santa Cruz de Tenerife, Spain

Fellow Honoris Causa, The Royal Incorporation of Architects, Scotland

Honorary Member of Colegio de Arquitectos, Mexico City

Maître d'Œuvre, Grande halle de la gare TGV Lyon–Saint-Exupéry Airport, Rhône, France

1995   *Santiago Calatrava*, exhibition, Centro Cultural de Belem, Lisbon

Santiago Calatrava—Construction and Movement, exhibition, Fondazione Angelo Masieri, Venice

Doctor Honoris Causa of Science, University College, Salford, England

Santiago Calatrava, exhibition, Navarra Museum, Pamplona, Spain

Award for Good Building 1983–1993, Canton of Lucerne, for the station and square

Certificate for the Practice of Professional Engineering, Frosinone, Italy

1996   Medalla de Oro al Mérito de las Bellas Artes, Ministry of Culture, Granada, Spain

Santiago Calatrava, exhibition, Archivo Foral, Bilbao, Spain

Santiago Calatrava, Bewegliche Architekturen—Bündel Fächer Welle, exhibition, Museum of Design, Zurich

Santiago Calatrava—opere e progetti 1980–1996, exhibition, Palazzo della Ragione, Padua, Italy

Mostra internazionale di scultura all'aperto, exhibition, Vira Gambarogno, Ascona, and Bellinzona, Italy

Doctor Honoris Causa of Science, University of Strathclyde, Glasgow, Scotland

Santiago Calatrava—Quatro Ponte sul Canal Grande, exhibition, Spazio Olivetti, Venice

Santiago Calatrava—Sculpture, exhibition, Government Building, St. Gallen, Switzerland

Santiago Calatrava—Kunst ist Bau—Bau ist Kunst, exhibition, Department of Building, Basel, Switzerland

Santiago Calatrava, exhibition, Milwaukee Art Museum, Milwaukee

Santiago Calatrava—City Point, *A New Tower for the City*, exhibition, Britannic Tower, London

1997   Doctor Honoris Causa of Science, Institute of Technology, Delft, The Netherlands

Santiago Calatrava—Structure and Movement, exhibition, National Museum of Science, Haifa, Israel

European Award for Steel Structures, reconstruction of the Kronprinzenbrücke, Berlin

Louis Vuitton–Moët Hennessy Art Prize, Paris

Master de Oro del Forum de Alta Dirección, Madrid

Doctor Honoris Causa of Engineering, Milwaukee School of Engineering, Milwaukee, Wisconsin

Structural Engineer License by the State of Illinois Department of Professional Engineering, License No. 081-005441, granted November (renewed in 1998 and 2000)

Temporary License for the Practice of Professional Engineering by the State of California Board of Professional Engineers and Land Surveyors (renewed in 1998)

1998   Member of *Les Arts et Lettres*, Paris

Santiago Calatrava—Work in Progress, exhibition, Triennale, Milan

Brunel Award, Madrid—Station d'Oriente, Lisbon Multimodal Station, Lisbon

Lecture series for the School of Architecture and Design at Massachusetts Institute of Technology, Cambridge, Massachusetts

Lecture series, winter semester, Architecture Department, ETH, Zurich

1999   Doctor Honoris Causa of Civil Engineering, Università degli Studi di Cassino, Cassino, Italy

Honorary Member of the Real Academia de Bellas Artes de San Fernando, Madrid

Príncipe de Asturias Art Prize, Spain

Doctor Honoris Causa of Technology, Lund University, Lund, Sweden

Foreign Member of the Academy, Royal Swedish Academy of Engineering Sciences, IVA

1999   License for the Practice of Professional Engineering by the State of Texas, Board of Professional Engineers, License No. 85263

Grau Grande Oficial da Ordem do Mérito, Chancelaria das Ordens Honorificas Portuguesas, Lisbon

Honorary Member of the Colegio de Ingenieros Técnicos de Obras Públicas, Madrid

Gold Medal, The Concrete Society, London

Canadian Consulting Engineering Awards, Honorable Mention, for the Mimico Creek Bridge, Toronto

2000   *Santiago Calatrava*, traveling exhibition, Montevideo, Uruguay, and Buenos Aires, Argentina

Doctor Honoris Causa of Architecture, Università degli Studi di Ferrara, Ferrara, Italy

Honorary Fellowship, Royal Architectural Institute of Canada College of Fellows, Ottawa

"Das Goldene Dach 2000" (The Golden Roof), Structural Completion of the Pfalzkeller, St. Gallen, Switzerland

Fellowship, Institute for Urban Design, New York

Honorary Fellowship, National Academy of Architecture, Monterrey, Mexico

Lecture series for the School of Architecture and Design at Massachusetts Institute of Technology, Cambridge, Massachusetts

Guest of Honor, Mexico City

Santiago Calatrava Scultore, Ingegnere, Architetto, exhibition, Palazzo Strozzi, Florence, Italy

Beauty and Efficiency, a Challenge of Modern Infrastructure, The IVA Royal Technology Forum, Stockholm

2000 Algur H. Meadows Award for Excellence in the Arts, Meadows School of Arts, Dallas

Temporary Licence and Certificate of Practice for Engineering, OAA, Ontario Association of Architects, Canada

Gold Medal, Círculo de Bellas Artes, Valencia

Honorary Academician, Real Academia de Bellas Artes de San Fernando, Madrid

2001   Prize Exitos 2000 for the best architectural work, for the Science Museum in Valencia, Madrid

       Calatrava: Architect, Sculptor, Engineer, exhibition, National Gallery Alexandros Soutzos Museum, Athens

       Calatrava: Poetics of Movement, exhibition, Meadows Museum, Southern Methodist University, Dallas

       Award for Excellence in Design for the *New York Times* Capsule, American Museum of Natural History,
       New York

       Temporary License for the Practice of Professional Engineering by the State of Wisconsin Board of Architects,
       Landscape Architects, Professional Engineers, Designers and Land Surveyors

       Santiago Calatrava Esculturas y Dibujos, exhibition, IVAM Centre Julio González, Valencia

       Calatrava XX/XXI, exhibition, Form and Design Center, Malmö, Sweden

       European Award for Steel Structures for the Europe Bridge over the Loire River, Orléans, France

       Calatrava, exhibition, Teloglion Foundation, Thessaloniki, Greece

2002   Best of 2001 Prize for the design of the Milwaukee Art Museum Extension, *Time*, New York

       "Il Principe e l'Architetto," prize for the design of the Quarto Ponte sul Canal Grande in Venice,
       Architettura e Design per la Città, Bologna, Italy

       Sir Misha Black Medal, Royal College of Art, London

       Prize 2002 The Best Large Structural Project for the Milwaukee Art Museum Addition,
       The Structural Engineers Association of Illinois

       Santiago Calatrava, traveling exhibition, Palacio de la Minería, Mexico City, and Museo de Arte Moderno,
       Santo Domingo, Dominican Republic

       Leonardo da Vinci Medal for outstanding contribution to international engineering education,
       SEFIRENZE 2000, Florence, Italy

2003   Medalla al Mérito a las Bellas Artes, Real Academia de San Carlos de Valencia, Valencia

Grande Médaille d'Or, Architecture, Académie d'Architecture, Paris

The European Steel Design Award for the Roof of the University of Zurich

The Silver Beam Award of the Swedish Institute of Steel Construction, Gothenburg, Sweden

The Illuminating Design Award of Merit of the Illuminating Engineering Society of North America, New York

Santiago Calatrava: Like a Bird, exhibition, Kunsthistorisches Museum, Vienna, Austria

2004   *WTC Project*, exhibition, Museum of Modern Art, New York

Golden Plate Award, Academy of Achievement, Chicago

Doctor Scientiarium Honoris Causa, Technion Israel Institute of Technology, Haifa, Israel

Tall Buildings, exhibition, Museum of Modern Art, New York

The Architect's Studio, exhibition, Henry Art Gallery, Seattle, Washington

Catalogue Raisonné

Cable-Stayed Bridge Studies
1979 Studies at ETH, Zurich

Letten Motorway Bridge
Zurich, Switzerland
1982 Project

Acleta Alpine Motor Bridge
Disentis, Switzerland
1979 Studies at ETH, Zurich

Schwarzhaupt Factory
Dielsdorf, Switzerland
1982 Project

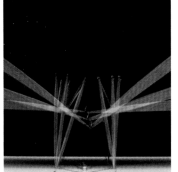

Roof for the IBA Squash Hall
Berlin, Germany
1979 Project

Mühlenareal Library
Thun, Switzerland
1982 Project

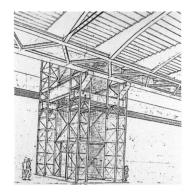

Züspa Exhibition Hall
Zurich, Switzerland
1981 Project

Rhine Bridge
Diepoldsau, Switzerland
1982 Project

Thalberg House Balcony Extension
Zurich, Switzerland
1983

Stadelhofen Railway Station
Zurich, Switzerland
1983–90

Jakem Warehouse
Münchwilen, Switzerland
1983–84

PTT Postal Center
Lucerne, Switzerland
1983–85

Ernsting Warehouse
Coesfeld-Lette, Germany
1983–85

St. Fiden Bus Shelter
St. Gallen, Switzerland
1983–85

Baumwollhof Balcony
Zurich, Switzerland
1983

Wohlen High School
Wohlen, Switzerland
1983–88

Lucerne Station Hall
Lucerne, Switzerland
1983–89

Caballeros Footbridge
Lerida, Spain
1985 Project

Bärenmatte Community Center
Suhr, Switzerland
1984–88

Bach de Roda Bridge
Barcelona, Spain
1985–87

Dobi Office Building
Suhr, Switzerland
1984–85

Feldenmoos Park & Ride Footbridge
Feldenmoos, Switzerland
1985 Project

De Sede Collapsible Exhibition Pavilion
Zurich, Switzerland
1984

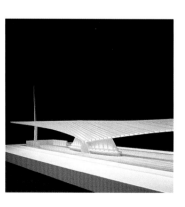

Station Square Bus Terminal
Lucerne, Switzerland
1985 Project

Avenida Diagonal Traffic Signal Gantry
Barcelona, Spain
1986

Tabourettli Theater
Basel, Switzerland
1986–87

9 d'Octubre Bridge
Valencia, Spain
1986–88

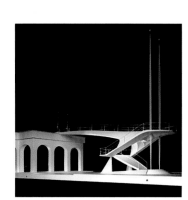

Raitenau Overpass
Salzburg, Austria
1986 Project

St. Gallen Music School Concert Room
St. Gallen, Switzerland
1986

BCE Place
Toronto, Canada
1987–92

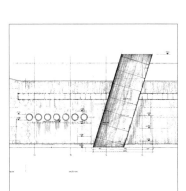

Blackbox Television Studio
Zurich, Switzerland
1986–87

Oudry-Mesly Footbridge
Créteil-Paris, France
1987–88

Thiers Pedestrian Bridge
Thiers, France
1987 Project

Buchen Housing Estate
Würenlingen, Switzerland
1987–96

Pontevedra Bridge
Pontevedra, Spain
1987 Project

Banco Exterior
Zurich, Switzerland
1987

Basarrate Metro Station
Bilbao, Spain
1987 Project

Cascine Footbridge
Florence, Italy
1987 Project

Alamillo Bridge
Seville, Spain
1987–92

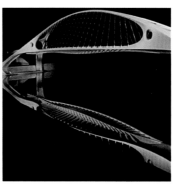

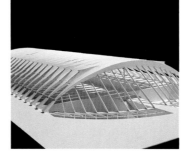

Pré Babel Sports Center
Geneva, Switzerland
1988 Project

Leimbach Footbridge and Station
Zurich, Switzerland
1988 Project

Gentil Bridge
Paris, France
1988 Project

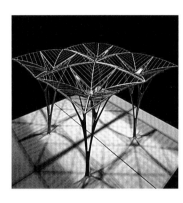

Lusitania Bridge
Mérida, Spain
1988–91

Bauschänzli Restaurant
Zurich, Switzerland
1988 Project

Collserola Communications Tower
Barcelona, Spain
1988 Project

Emergency Services Center
St. Gallen, Switzerland
1988–98

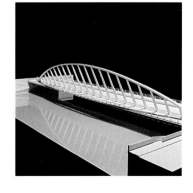

Wettstein Bridge
Basel, Switzerland
1988 Project

Miraflores Bridge
Cordoba, Spain
1989 Project

Montjuic Communications Tower
Barcelona, Spain
1989–92

Bohl Bus and Tram Stop
St. Gallen, Switzerland
1989–96

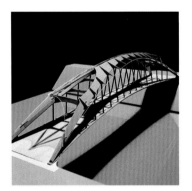

Bahnhofquai Tram Stop
Zurich, Switzerland
1989 Project

Zurich University Law Faculty
Zurich, Switzerland
1989–2004

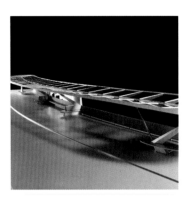

Reuss Footbridge
Flüelen, Switzerland
1989 Project

Muri Cloister Old Age Home
Muri, Switzerland
1989 Project

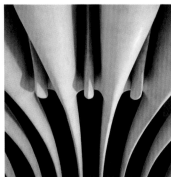

Swissbau Pavilion
Basel, Switzerland
1988

Lyons Airport Station
Satolas (Lyons), France
1989–94

CH-91 Pavilion
Lucerne, Switzerland
1989 Project

Port de la Lune Swingbridge
Bordeaux, France
1989 Project

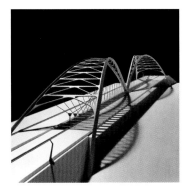

Gran Via Bridge
Barcelona, Spain
1989 Project

Volantin Footbridge
Bilbao, Spain
1990–97

Puerto Bridge
Ondarroa, Spain
1989–91

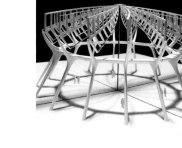

Spitalfields Gallery
London, England
1990 Project

La Devesa Footbridge
Ripoll, Spain
1989–91

East London River Crossing
London, England
1990 Project

New Bridge over the Vecchio
Corsica, France
1990 Project

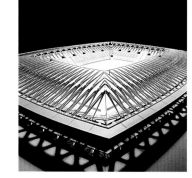

Calabria Football Stadium
Reggio Calabria, Italy
1991 Project

Belluard Castle Theater
Fribourg, Switzerland
1990 Project

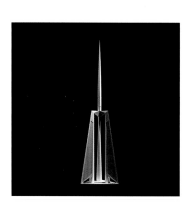

Valencia Communications Tower
Valencia, Spain
1991 Project

Sondica Airport
Bilbao, Spain
1990–2000

Kuwait Pavilion
Seville, Spain
1991–92

Tenerife Concert Hall
Tenerife, Canary Islands, Spain
1991–2003

Salou Football Stadium
Salou, Spain
1991 Project

City of Arts and Sciences
Valencia, Spain
1991–96

Médoc Swingbridge
Bordeaux, France
1991 Project

Grand Pont
Lille, France
1991 Project

Kronprinzen Bridge
Berlin, Germany
1991–96

Alameda Bridge and Underground Station
Valencia, Spain
1991–95

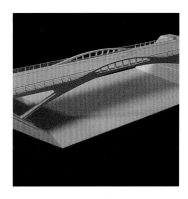

Beton Forum Standard Bridge
Stockholm, Sweden
1991 Project

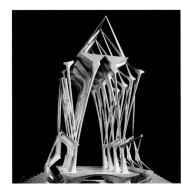

Cathedral of St. John the Divine
New York City
1991 Project

Spandau Station
Berlin, Germany
1991 Project

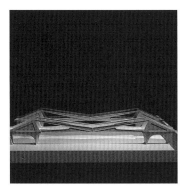

Klosterstrasse Railway Viaduct
Berlin, Germany
1991 Project

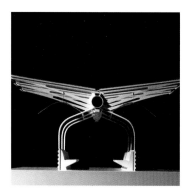

Modular Station
London, England
1992 Project

Oberbaum Bridge
Berlin, Germany
1991–96

Tenerife Exhibition Center
Tenerife, Canary Islands, Spain
1992–95

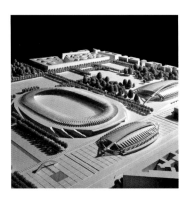

Jahn Olympic Sports Complex
Berlin, Germany
1991 Project

Reichstag
Berlin, Germany
1992 Project

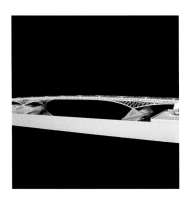

Solferino Footbridge
Paris, France
1992 Project

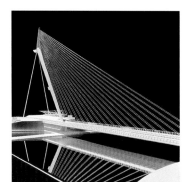

Serreria Bridge
Valencia, Spain
1992–

Lake Bridge
Lucerne, Switzerland
1992 Project

Ile Falcon Viaduct
Sierre, Switzerland
1993 Project

Alcoy Community Hall
Alcoy, Spain
1992–95

Trinity Footbridge
Salford, England
1993–95

Serpis Bridge
Alcoy, Spain
1992 Project

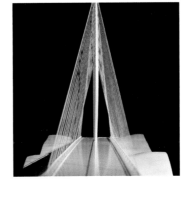

Granadilla Bridge
Tenerife, Canary Islands, Spain
1993 Project

Öresund Link
Copenhagen, Denmark
1993 Project

De la Rade Bridge
Geneva, Switzerland
1993 Project

Alicante Communications Tower
Alicante, Spain
1993 Project

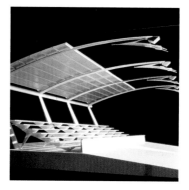

Herne Hill Stadium
London, England
1993 Project

Hospital Bridges
Murcia, Spain
1993–99

Oriente Station
Lisbon, Portugal
1993–98

Sondica Airport Control Tower
Bilbao, Spain
1993–96

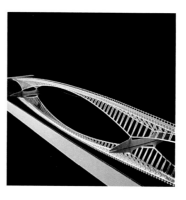

St. Paul's Footbridge
London, England
1994 Project

Manrique Footbridge
Murcia, Spain
1994–99

Quaypoint Pedestrian Bridge
Bristol, England
1994 Project

Sundial Bridge
Redding, California
1995–2003

Milwaukee Art Museum
Milwaukee, Wisconsin
1994–2001

Zurich Station Roof
Zurich, Switzerland
1995 Project

**Michelangelo Trade Fair
and Convention Center**
Fiuggi, Italy
1994 Project

KL Linear City
Kuala Lumpur, Malaysia
1995 Project

Velodrome Football Stadium
Marseilles, France
1995 Project

Poole Harbour Bridge
Portsmouth, England
1995 Project

Embankment Renaissance Footbridge
Bedford, England
1995 Project

Olympic Stadium
Stockholm, Sweden
1996 Project

Sundsvall Bridge
Sundsvall, Sweden
1995 Project

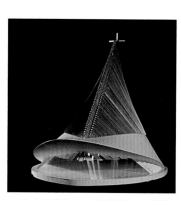

Church of the Year 2000
Rome, Italy
1996 Project

Bilbao Football Stadium
Bilbao, Spain
1995 Project

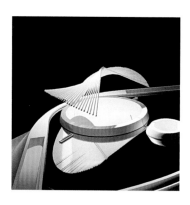

Cathedral Square
Los Angeles, California
1996 Project

Quarto Ponte sul Canal Grande
Venice, Italy
1996–

City Point
London, England
1996 Project

Mimico Creek Pedestrian Bridge
Toronto, Canada
1996–98

Pont d'Orléans
Orléans, France
1996–2000

Valencia Opera House
Valencia, Spain
1996–2004

Port de Barcelona
Barcelona, Spain
1997 Project

Porte de la Suisse Motorway Service Area
Geneva, Switzerland
1996 Project

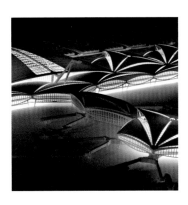

Barajas Airport
Madrid, Spain
1997 Project

Liège Guillemins TGV Railway Station
Liège, Belgium
1996–

Pfalzkeller Gallery
St. Gallen, Switzerland
1988–98

Pennsylvania Station
New York City
1998 Project

La Rioja Bodegas Ysios Winery
La Guardia, Spain
1998–2001

Pont des Guillemins
Liège, Belgium
1998–2000

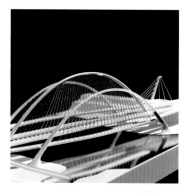

Woodall Rodgers Bridge City Project
(Trinity River Bridge)
Dallas, Texas
1998–2006

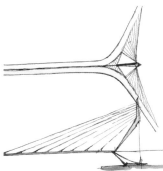

Petach-Tikva Footbridge
Petach-Tikva, Israel
1998–2003

Puente de la Mujer
Buenos Aires, Argentina
1998–2001

Toronto Island Airport Bridge
Toronto, Canada
1998 Project

James Joyce Bridge
Dublin, Ireland
1998–2003

Wildbachstrasse
Zurich, Switzerland
1999

Nova Ponte Sobre o Rio Cavado
Barcelos, Portugal
1999 Project

Corcoran Gallery of Art
Washington, D.C.
1999 Project

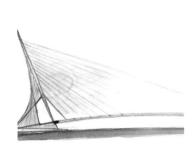

Pedestrian Bridge
Pistoia, Italy
1999 Project

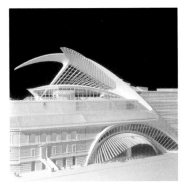

Turning Torso Apartment Tower
Malmö, Sweden
1999–2005

Rouen Bridge
Rouen, France
1999 Project

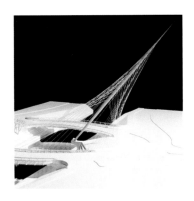

Bridges over the Hoofdvaart
Hoofddorp, Netherlands
1999–2004

Cruz y Luz
Monterrey, Mexico
1999 Project

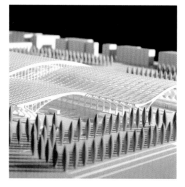

Zaragoza Station
Zaragoza, Spain
1999 Project

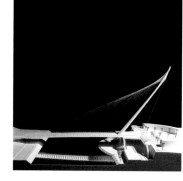

Ponte sul Crati
Cosenza, Italy
2000–

Residence
Phoenix, Arizona
1999 Project

Christ the Light Cathedral
Oakland, California
2000 Project

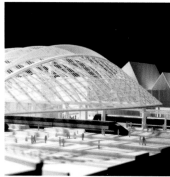

Leuven Station
Sint-Niklaas, Belgium
1999 Project

Opera House Parking
Zurich, Switzerland
2000 Project

Reina Sofia National Museum of Art
Madrid, Spain
1999 Project

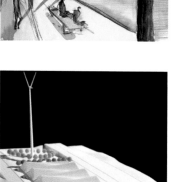
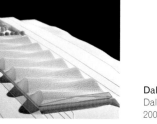

Dallas–Fort Worth Airport
Dallas, Texas
2000 Project

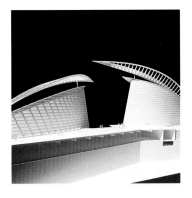

Buenavista y Jovellanos
Oviedo, Spain
2000–

Stadium Zurich
Zurich, Switzerland
2000 Project

Ryerson Polytechnic University
Toronto, Canada
2000 Project

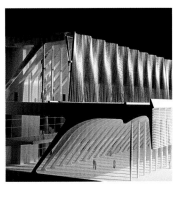

Ciudad de la Porcelana
Valencia, Spain
2000–

Darsena del Puerto, Centro Municipal
Torrevieja, Spain
2000 Project

University Campus Buildings
and Sports Hall
Maastricht, Netherlands
2000–

Kornhaus
Rorschach, Switzerland
2000–

American Museum of Natural History
New York City
2001 Project

Queens Landing Pedestrian
Access Improvement
Chicago, Illinois
2001 Project

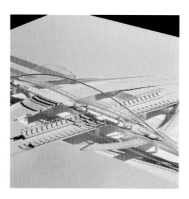

Neratziotissa Metro and Railway Station
Athens, Greece
2001–

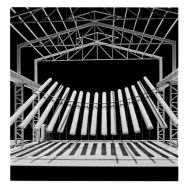

Stage Setting for *Las Troyanas*
Valencia, Spain
2001–

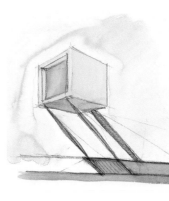

Residence
Qatar, Qatar
2001–

Master Plan for the 2004 Olympic
and Paralympic Games
Athens, Greece
2001–4

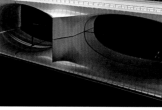

Bridge of Vittoria
Florence, Italy
2002 Project

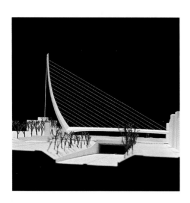

Katehaki Pedestrian Bridge
Athens, Greece
2001–4

Expansion for the Museo dell'Opera
del Duomo
Florence, Italy
2002–

Reggio Emilia
Reggio Emilia, Italy
2002–

Nuova Stazione
Florence, Italy
2003 Project

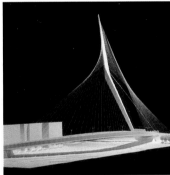

Stage Setting for *Ecuba*
Rome, Italy
2002–

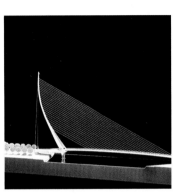

Greenpoint Landing
New York City
2002 Project

Light Rail Train Bridge
Jerusalem, Israel
2002–

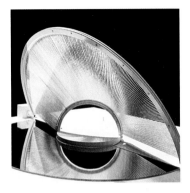

80 South Street Tower
New York City
2000–

Atlanta Symphony Orchestra
Concert Hall
Atlanta, Georgia
2002–

World Trade Center Transportation Hub
New York City
2003–

Photography Credits

Sergio Belinchón: 222

Jim Brozek: 292–93, 300, 301

Barbara Burg and Oliver Schuh: 2–3, 6–7, 8–9, 12–13, 51, 67, 69, 78–79, 82, 87, 89, 92, 93, 101, 108, 178, 181, 182, 189, 191, 192, 193, 197, 198–99, 200, 201, 217, 224, 225, 242, 243 top, 249, 288, 305, 311, 314

Santiago Calatrava Archive: 306–7

Christophe Demonfaucon: Jacket back, 18–19, 316, 317, 318–19

Todd Eberle: 337, 338, 339, 340–41, 342, 343, 344, 345

Hans Ege: 167, 168 top, 169

Roland Halbe: 323, 324–25, 326, 327

Heinrich Helfenstein: 157, 163, 171, 172, 173, 230, 231, 234, 235, 236, 237, 239, 253, 258, 260, 261, 276, 277, 281, 334, 335, 336, 347, 352, 353, 358, 359, 364, 367, 371, 376

Timothy Hursley: 295

Alan Karchmer: Jacket front, 10–11, 16–17, 20, 30–31, 38–39, 60–61, 112–13, 140–41, 203, 204, 205, 206, 208, 209, 250–51, 282–83, 291, 298, 299, 302–3, 328, 329, 330–31, 356–57, 372–73, 390–91, 408–9

New York Times: 268, 269

Peter Mauss/Esto: 95, 96–97

Paolo Rosselli: 4–5, 14–15, 43, 59, 70, 73, 77, 84, 85, 88, 90, 100, 105, 106–7, 111, 142, 143, 144, 147, 148, 152–53, 154, 159, 161, 165, 166, 168 bottom, 175, 176–77, 179, 180, 183, 185, 186–87, 194–95, 211, 212, 213, 227, 228–29, 241, 243 bottom, 245, 247, 263, 270, 271, 273, 274–75, 285, 286–87, 309

David Sundberg/Esto: 375, 377

Giorgio von Arb and Andreas Camenzind: 255, 256, 257, 262, 264, 265, 266–67, 272